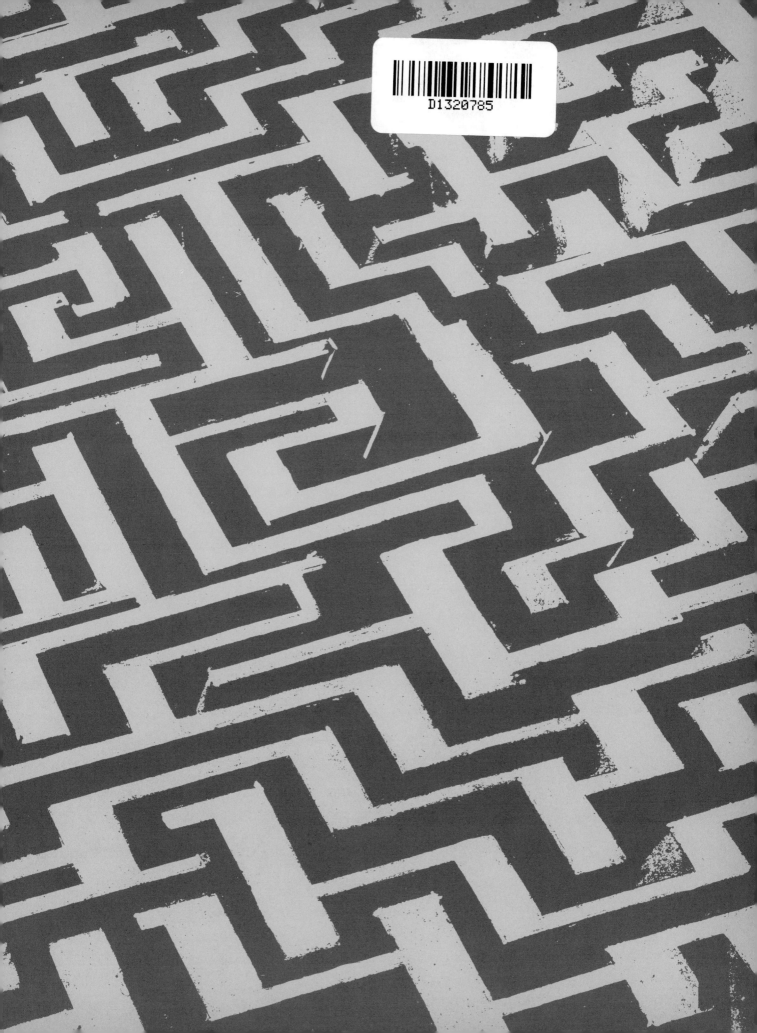

UFO:
THE CONTINUING
ENIGMA

QUEST FOR THE UNKNOWN

UFO:
THE CONTINUING
ENIGMA

Reader's
Digest

THE READER'S DIGEST ASSOCIATION LIMITED
London, New York, Montreal, Sydney, Cape Town

Quest for the Unknown
Created, edited, and designed by DK Direct Limited

A DORLING KINDERSLEY BOOK

First published 1992 in Great Britain by
The Reader's Digest Association Limited,
Berkeley Square House, Berkeley Square, London W1X 6AB,
in association with
Dorling Kindersley Limited,
9 Henrietta Street, Covent Garden, London

DK DIRECT LIMITED

Senior Editor Richard Williams
Editors Deirdre Headon, Sarah Miller
Editorial Research Julie Whitaker
Editorial Secretary Pat White

Senior Art Editor Simon Webb
Designer Mark Osborne
Picture Research Frances Vargo; **Picture Assistant** Sharon Southren

Editorial Director Jonathan Reed; **Design Director** Ed Day

Volume Consultants Hilary Evans, Reg Grant
Contributors Peter Brookesmith, Rusty Hudson, Kevin McClure, Jenny Randles,
John Rimmer, Dennis Stacy
Illustrators Paul Bailey, Russell Barnet, Roger Cherrill Ltd., Roy Flooks, Peter Gudynas,
Julek Heller, Imago, Richard Manning, Mark Surridge
Photographers Simon Farnhell, Andrew Griffin, Mark Hamilton,
Steve Jeffries, Steve Lyne, Susanna Price

A CIP catalogue record for this book is available from the British Library

ISBN 0 276 42061 6

Printed in Spain by Printer Industria Gráfica S.A.

FOREWORD

*S*TRANGE OBJECTS IN THE SKY have been seen all over the world since the dawn of recorded history. These sightings are often reported, not by dreamers or charlatans, but by ordinary, sensible people going about their business. Frightened and perplexed by their experiences, they are generally more embarrassed to relate them than they are eager for publicity.

Numerous theories have been put forth by way of explanation — some suggesting that extraterrestrial spacecraft are literal realities, others claiming that such phenomena are produced by the vast and unexplored powers of the human mind, still others holding that people who think they have seen flying saucers are mentally unstable. Finding a sensible path through the enormous mass of information and hypothesis is difficult; the "rational" interpretations offered by the skeptics often sound as farfetched as the most hysterical abductee reports involving glowing aliens and interplanetary travel.

This volume explores the latest findings of a wide range of experts in every relevant field, from meteorology to aeronautics. In all these areas, new ideas are being examined every day, and these investigations may eventually force us to expand our horizons and change some of our long-held beliefs. In the meantime, the best we can do is study the facts with an open mind. We must avoid the intellectual dead end of assuming that a particular phenomenon cannot exist simply because our present knowledge is incapable of explaining it.

— *The Editors*

CONTENTS

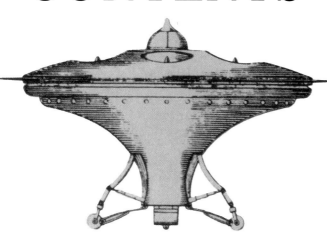

FOREWORD

UFO's THROUGH THE AGES

INTRODUCTION
AN ALIEN ENCOUNTER

INVESTIGATORS AND SPACECRAFT

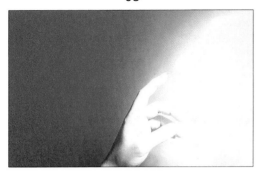

AN ALIEN ENCOUNTER

In recent years thousands of ordinary people have made extraordinary claims — that they have been abducted by aliens. What follows is the terrifying account of one such "abductee," a young musician named Rusty Hudson.

"Think of all the strange objects you find in the ancient Egyptian wing of a museum. The purpose of many of them is unfathomable. Then take that strangeness times a thousand — try to imagine a place designed and engineered by non-humans. It's almost impossible to describe. I know. I've been there.

"Although I may have had more than one encounter, I shall recount only the details of the most clear-cut experience. It occurred around June 21, 1980. I was then 23 years old, and had been on the road for six weeks with a pop band called Excalibur.

"We were playing in hotels and resorts and sending money home to pay off college loans. That week we were staying in a motel in the west Florida town of Plant City. Our actual job was in nearby Tampa, but after finishing each night at 1:00 A.M., we would drive back to our accommodation in Plant City. We had been in town a few days when the incident occurred.

"We had just completed our last set, and had arrived back at the motel. Usually, after entertaining people for four hours, we would be wide awake, and spend the rest of the night talking, reading books, hanging out at the pool, or going to an all-night diner. Drugs were not part of our band lifestyle. People who enjoyed our music would occasionally buy us a drink or two after a show, but we were pretty 'square' as bands go.

A flash of light
"On that particular night, I had dropped off my instrument in the room I was sharing with the bassist, and had gone to visit Mark and J., two other members of the group who were staying in an adjacent room.

"We were engrossed in conversation when we were suddenly disturbed by what looked like a brief, sputtering flash of light in the room. My first thought was that it must have been the glare of a passing car's headlights, but it wasn't. We were on the second floor of the motel and the curtains at the room's only window were closed. I quickly scanned the room for an explanation.

"It was a typical American motel room. The entrance was to my left, next to a large front window with the curtains drawn. Beyond the door was a balcony/walkway with entrances to the other rooms. I was leaning against a sort of vanity facing two double beds, between which was a night-stand with a lamp. Mark sat on the bed to my left, J. was reclining on the one to my right. There was a television to my immediate left

turned on but with the sound off, and a few paces to my right was a washbasin with a large mirror on the wall behind it. To the left of this was the bathroom. I remember saying, 'Did you see that?' and Mark and J. replying that they had.

"A few seconds later, something impossible happened. An intensely bright white light seemed to burst out of the back of the room by the mirror and washbasin as if someone had suddenly opened a door to the sun.

Insane, impossible...
"Then, in the midst of this glare I saw movement, and then two very large, slanted black eyes. Tiny pinpoints of reflected light seemed to swim in them. I do not know if I screamed. It was as if I was retreating into some safe place in my mind. What was occurring was insane, impossible. I was beginning to convince myself that I was hallucinating when I heard a strange sound.

"I turned, in what seemed like slow-motion, to see J.'s fear-contorted face screaming something. I turned further and saw Mark shaking as if in shock. I then turned back toward the light, in that same terrible slow-motion, and looked into a face that I will never forget as long as I live. A huge, pale head with enormous black, glistening eyes and an enigmatic Mona Lisa smile was coming toward me. I could not move. My head was filled with a sound that had been building in intensity since the light first appeared. It was a high-pitched buzzing, a hollow hum, not unlike the sound of a hornet's nest, but much louder. I looked into the eyes, then....

"I was sitting at the foot of my bed in my motel room, looking at a test pattern on the television. I was exhausted. I could not figure out how I had got back to my room. I could recall some strange images, but my weariness overpowered any train of thought and I was sound asleep almost instantly.

"I slept until late afternoon. When I finally got out of bed, I began to

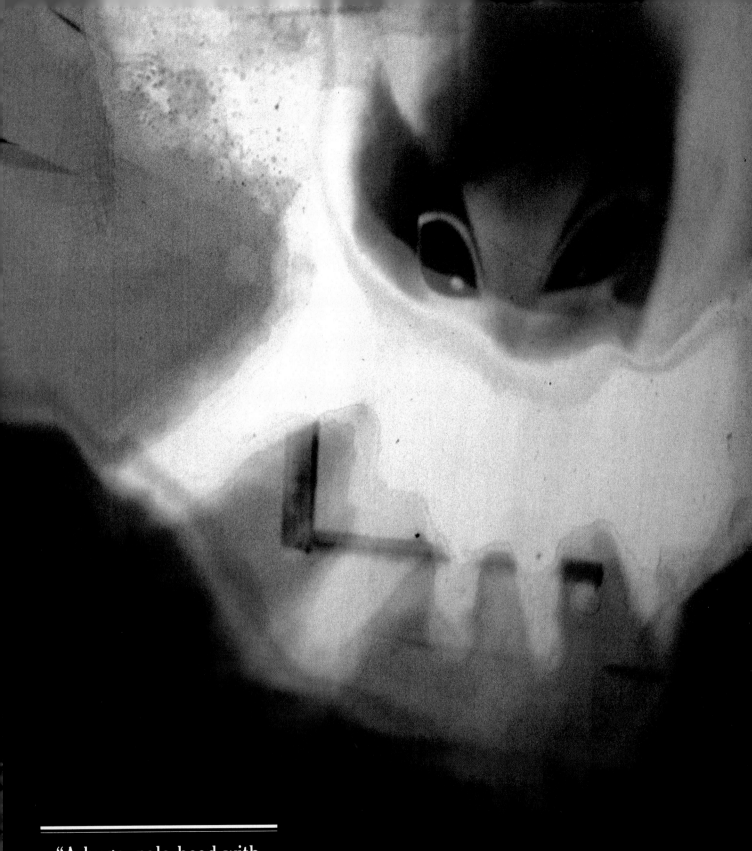

"A huge, pale head with enormous black, glistening eyes and an enigmatic Mona Lisa smile was coming toward me."

remember some of the previous night's events. I felt emotionally muted – a bit numb. I went and found J. and Mark in their room, which looked normal but which made me feel extremely nervous. I asked them if they remembered anything 'funny' from the night before. They looked at each other, then at me. J. said, 'You mean that light? That light that came out of the mirror?' I felt as

"A face just like the one I had been sketching for the last seven years."

though the floor was giving way – like the whole world was going hopelessly topsy-turvy. Mark said, 'Yeah. I saw it too.' There was a pause. J. said, 'I don't think we should talk about this.' Mark and I nodded in assent, and that was the end of it.

"Only it wasn't.

"In the years that followed I was plagued by recurring nightmares and insomnia. Over and over, I would wake up in the middle of the night in a panic, scanning the room for anything out of place. Sometimes I would get out of bed and look around the apartment, though I had no idea what I was looking for. I could no longer sleep on my back without suffering anxiety attacks. I began doodling a strange face with big black eyes on the margins of notebooks and newspapers. I felt as though I was waiting for something to happen.

Stories and sketches
"The band had broken up a few weeks after the incident. I eventually lost track of J. and seldom saw Mark. When we did see each other we avoided mentioning that night.

"A few years later, I returned to university life. I continued to sketch the face that haunted my dreams, and wrote short stories about strange

beings, bright lights, and inexplicable displacements. One Sunday morning in February 1987, a girlfriend of mine was over having brunch with me. I had told her my little story a year before and she had attributed it to my overactive imagination; she had often expressed distaste at my drawings of what she called 'that horrid face.'

"After eating, she was having a coffee and reading the *New York Times Book Review*, when she suddenly jumped up and almost dropped the paper. I looked up at her in surprise, and she slowly flipped the paper around to reveal a full-page book advertisement adorned with a face just like the one I had been sketching for the last seven years.

"Within days, I had both Budd Hopkins's book *Intruders* and Whitley Strieber's *Communion*. But, inexplicably, I could not bring myself to read either. Just looking at the pictures in *Intruders* or reading the first few pages of *Communion* would get me extremely agitated. This was odd because I am an avid reader. But something about these books really scared me. My girlfriend did read them and began urging me to contact Budd Hopkins. It took me a year to overcome my reluctance, but in the spring of 1988 I called him and agreed to come in for a preliminary interview.

Hypnotic regression
"Budd told me that my story and my 'symptoms' were highly indicative of a pattern. He then suggested that if I wished to look further into my experiences, that I should not read his books or any other UFO books, and, if I wished, I should undergo hypnotic regression. The purpose of this was to uncover what had happened in the missing-time interval between my gazing into the huge black eyes and finding myself back in my own motel room.

"He gave me the phone numbers of people who had already been through the process so that I could ask questions. The only subject not to be discussed was the content of their sessions: this for the same reason I was advised not to read the books, so that I could feel more certain that my memories were my own.

"Ultimately, I did agree to have my experiences investigated, and ended up working with Budd and two psychiatrists. The good news was that I wasn't crazy. After being questioned and tested, I was told that mentally and emotionally, I was basically healthy. The bad news was that, as hypnosis helped me piece together the events of the night, I was faced with a bizarre, unsettling story, and the growing certainty that my memories were real.

"What follows is an excerpt from the transcripts of one of my sessions of hypnotic regression:

(In the course of this session, the psychiatrist brought me back to the night of the incident. I described the room, the light, and the arrival of the being, then became upset.)

PSYCHIATRIST: What made you cry?
RUSTY: (Very long pause.) (Gasps.) I remember. J. is really scared, and he said, 'I won't let them take you.' (Long pause.) I think he's really scared. And I'm really scared. I wish I could say to him, 'Don't be scared.'
P: Why are you scared?
R: Because I'm thinking that the face at the mirror is something in my mind, but then I'm starting to think it's real. And when I start thinking it's real I start shaking and I think, 'No, no, no.' You know?
P: 'No, no' what?
R: Ugh, I....It's coming closer and I don't want it to, and I'm saying 'No. No. No.' (Long pause.) But I'm not doing anything! And the face seems very close. I'm almost eye-to-eye. It's almost...it's scary...it's almost like a skull. It seems like it's smiling but it's like it couldn't have any other expression than what it has.
P: What about it is scaring you? What about it is scary?

R: Because...the power of it is so overwhelming. I can't do anything. I feel like it could just blow me up or it could hurt me and I can't do anything about it.
P: Is that when you start crying?
R: (Tears welling up.) I start crying because I'm thinking I'm seeing something that's just an image in the mirror. And I look again and it's standing there and it can't be standing there. I mean, how could it be standing there? (Angry.) Things just don't come out of mirrors or appear in your room. And it just keeps smiling. It doesn't say anything. It's just looking at me. And J.'s going 'Oh, my God!' And J., he went over and he's crawling on the floor and he's grabbing my ankle of my left foot...like I could protect him. Like I would know what to do. I...I...I don't know if this is real.
P: We'll sort it out later. Just tell me what it feels like.
R: It's standing there. It's all white. It's pale. It has a big head. The thing I just keep looking at is the eyes, though. And how thin the legs are...arms are very thin.
P: How big is this?
R: It's not as big as me. It's like...it's a little bit shorter than me. Maybe like an 11-year-old kid or something like that.

A medical examination
"Later in the session, I described lying on my back on a hard surface in a dark room with bright lights shining down into my face. I felt as though I was being poked and prodded along my right side.

"Then, suddenly, I felt something cold touch my right arm and the right side of my chest. Almost instantly, my body was flooded with a cool, tingling sensation. I felt extremely relaxed and astonishingly unafraid. I indistinctly saw some sort of large black apparatus brought over my chest. I felt groggy, as if drugged.

"The rest of the experience consisted of a medical examination, although the procedures were unlike any I've ever

heard about. In fact, the one generalization I could make about the 'alien' environment is that it was completely and totally alien. Nothing was recognizable. It was very difficult for me to get my perceptual bearings.

A thin scar

"Toward the end of the experience I felt a very sharp pain in my left knee. It seemed to throb for quite a while and I compared it to the sensation of a typhoid inoculation delivered by air gun. When the hypnotic session was over, the psychiatrist asked me if I had any unusual marks or scars in the area of my leg where I had felt the pain. I said no. However, the following morning at home, I decided to make a close inspection just to put my mind at ease. To my horror, I discovered a thin, but well-defined scar, about an inch long, in a vertical line just above my knee cap.

"I felt dizzy. Budd was on vacation, so I called one of the people he had suggested I contact in the event of a crisis. When I described the scar, he asked me to come to his house as soon as possible. He took a look at my scar and said, 'You're not going to like this.' He pulled up his pants leg and showed me a scar above his left knee that was virtually identical to mine -- in the same position, even at the same angle.

"In order to honor the agreement we had made with Budd, I didn't ask for details of his experience, though he did tell me that, like me, he could not remember getting a deep cut above his knee in any conventional manner.

"Ultimately, the process of retrieving the forgotten material brought me some emotional relief. I was not crazy about the idea of these beings, whoever or whatever they are, snatching me out of a motel room for mysterious medical

experiments. But they had not seriously harmed me, and now that I could remember many of the features and details of my previously nameless fears, I could sleep again.

"Parts of the incident remain obscure. I still do not know how I got from Mark and J.'s motel room to that strange place I was taken to. I have finally concluded that I must have lost consciousness at some point. The trip back seemed to take only seconds. I now remember entering a small, round room filled with blue light, a tingling sensation, the feeling of rapid movement, and suddenly finding myself standing at my motel room door in a complete daze.

Eyewitness testimony

"I recently contacted Mark, and finally asked him what he remembered about that evening. He recalled the strange bright light and what he described as a 'jump in time.' One moment, J. was sitting on the bed and I was by the vanity. The next, J. was on the floor, and I was no longer where I had been. Again, I was forced to confront evidence which indicated that my memories are of actual events.

"Often, I find all of this too overwhelming and either put it out of my mind, or try to convince myself that it never happened. But then I will suddenly, and vividly, remember a moment of the experience, or I will hear another 'abductee' mention, matter-of-factly, an aspect of the experience I've never discussed with anyone.

"Writing this article has been extremely difficult for me. This has been a bit surprising because in the normal course of events I really enjoy writing. Some of my hesitation is, I suppose, easy to understand. Going public with a story like this is bound to raise a few eyebrows among my associates. I am an Ivy League-educated professional musician living in New York City. My reputation is important to me. I should also like to protect my family and friends from the sort of questionable publicity such disclosures generate.

"In addition to all of this, I feel extremely uncomfortable dredging this material up. Yet, here I am, writing this article. A cynic might suggest that I am doing it for the money. Rest assured. By the time you read this, my modest commission will have been applied to part of my monthly rent. Well, what about all the possible publicity? I ask you. Would you want to be well known for describing a bizarre and disturbing UFO experience? I would much prefer to be known and appreciated for my talents — not as a UFO case, an oddity.

"I am writing this article because, as far as I can establish, these seemingly incredible experiences really happened. They do not fit in with the rest of my life; yet I am left with terrifyingly vivid memories, the corroborative accounts of those who were there with me, and some physical evidence.

Frightened and confused people

"This is not an isolated incident. I have met dozens of people whose experiences parallel mine in incredible detail. I have seen letters from hundreds more, and I now suspect that there are perhaps tens of thousands of frightened and confused people out there who still do not know what happened to them. I am writing this for them — not because I claim to understand this phenomenon, but because the only hope that it will ever be understood lies in our refusal to continue denying its existence. Only then can we get down to the business of learning who or what has decided to embark on this strange relationship with us. "

Rusty Hudson
August 1990

> "The trip back seemed to take only seconds. I now remember entering a small, round room filled with blue light, a tingling sensation, the feeling of rapid movement, and suddenly finding myself standing at my motel room door in a complete daze."

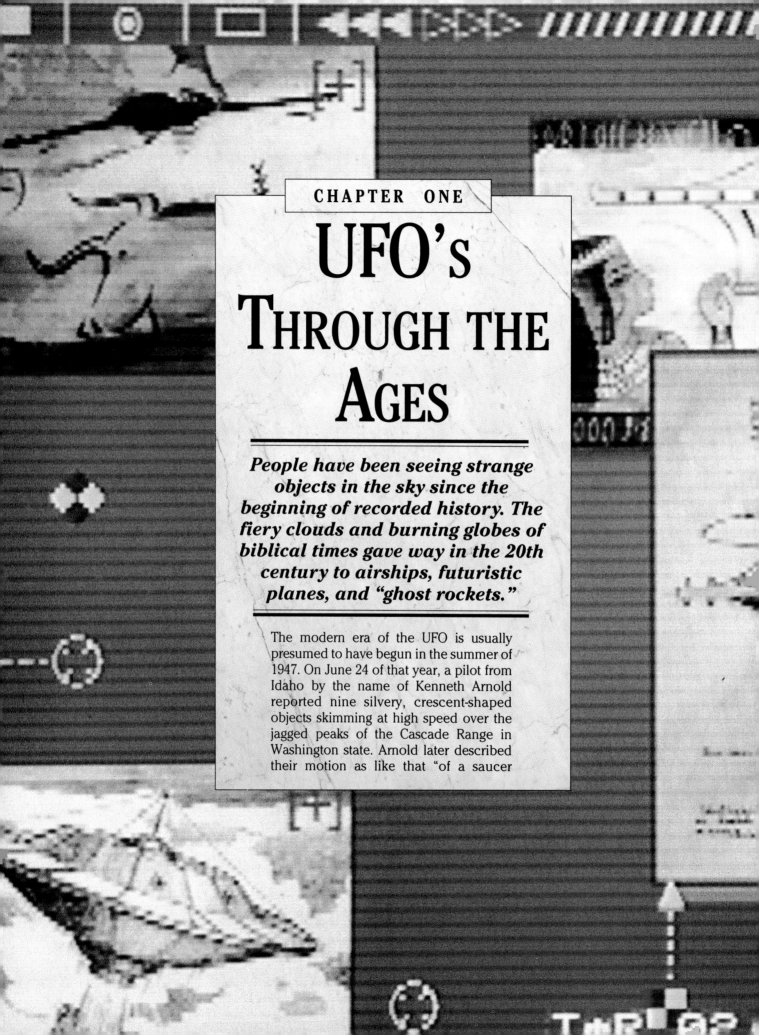

CHAPTER ONE

UFO's THROUGH THE AGES

People have been seeing strange objects in the sky since the beginning of recorded history. The fiery clouds and burning globes of biblical times gave way in the 20th century to airships, futuristic planes, and "ghost rockets."

The modern era of the UFO is usually presumed to have begun in the summer of 1947. On June 24 of that year, a pilot from Idaho by the name of Kenneth Arnold reported nine silvery, crescent-shaped objects skimming at high speed over the jagged peaks of the Cascade Range in Washington state. Arnold later described their motion as like that "of a saucer

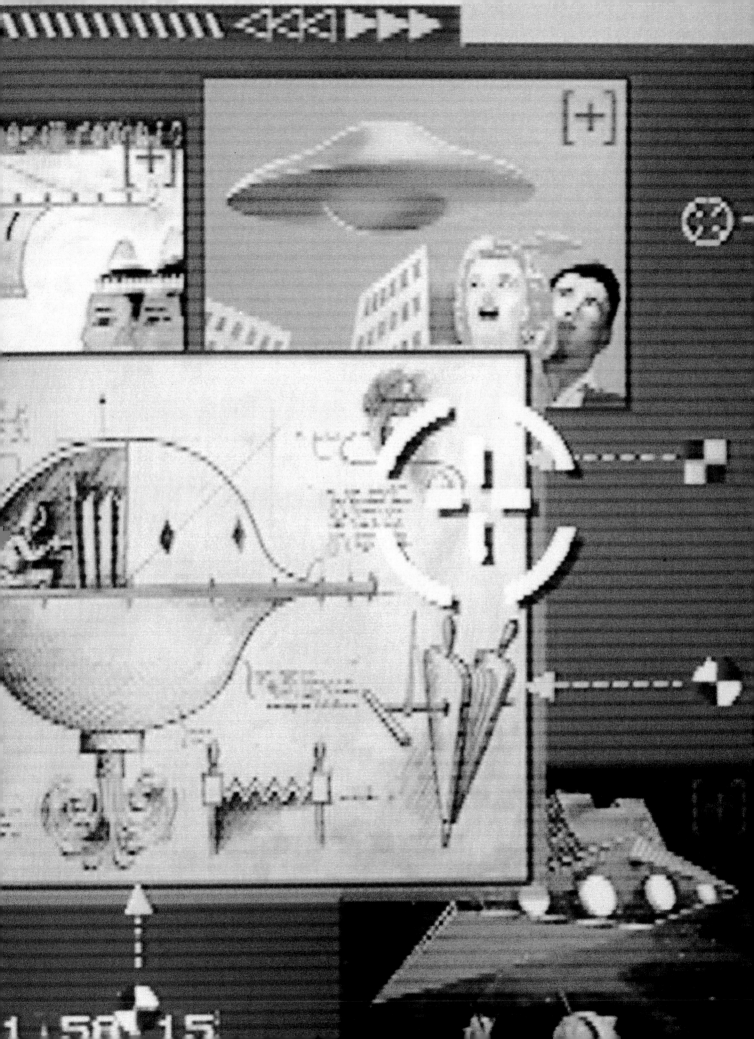

15th century *B.C.*
Egypt
The annals of pharaoh Thutmose III tell of foul-smelling circles of fire and flying discs in the sky.

skipping over water." An Associated Press reporter shortened the phrase to "flying saucers," and the rest, as they say, is history.

The heavens, it appears, have always been haunted by UFO's, or at least since there have been human observers to record them. The French ufologist and author Aimé Michel, for example, points to a series of paleolithic Cro-Magnon cave paintings scattered throughout

Europe that date to about 20,000 B.C. Some appear to portray objects similar in shape to the Apollo module that first landed American astronauts on the moon, complete with antenna and landing struts. Among the bison, deer, and mammoths of the famous Altamira cave paintings in Spain are similar shapes, at least one with what seems to be a figure standing alongside. Are these crude line drawings the first evidence of

6th century *B.C.*
Mesopotamia
The prophet Ezekiel said he saw four beings of human appearance emerge from a vessel of bronze.

A.D. **747**
China
Huge, flame-breathing dragons were reported flying in the sky, followed by men in airships.

A.D. **900**
Lyon, France
Three men and a woman were reported leaving an aerial ship and being set upon by a mob.

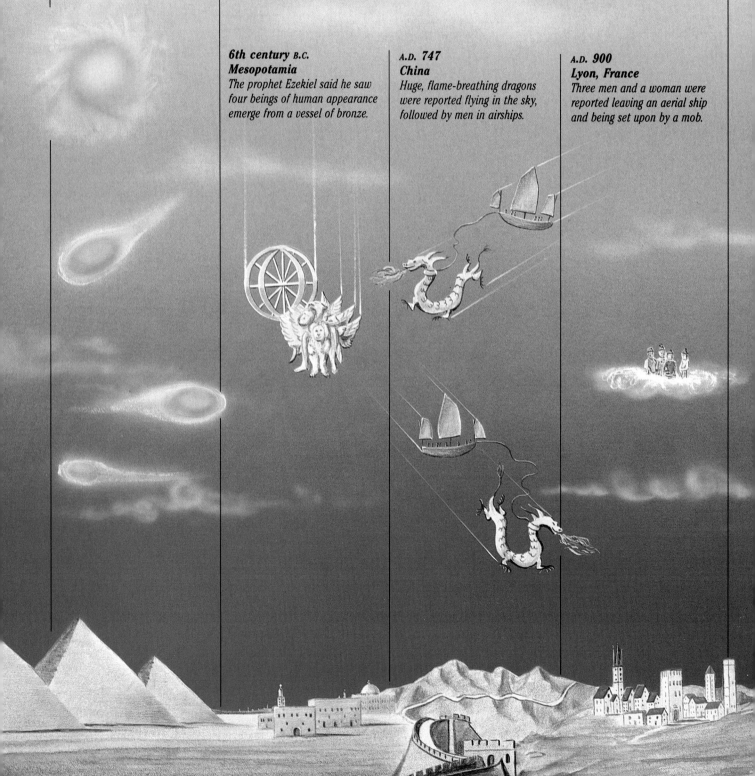

extraterrestrial visitors? Or are they merely the artistic rendering of ancient magical symbols?

Raining fishes and birds

An Egyptian papyrus, said to be a 3,400-year-old fragment of the *Annals of Thutmose III*, may contain the first written account of a UFO. The papyrus describes numerous nocturnal "fire circles" that "shone more in the sky than the brightness of the sun." Rising high in the south, the fiery circles rained down "fishes and winged creatures...a marvel never before known since the foundation of the land." The pharaoh ordered incense burned, and the event recorded for future posterity.

The two great epic religious poems of India, the *Mahabharata* and *Ramayana*, written around 2,000 years ago, both mention disc-like military flying

◆ PAGE 24

April 1897
Le Roy, Kansas
A bizarre sighting was reported of an airship rising and trailing a heifer tied to a red rope.

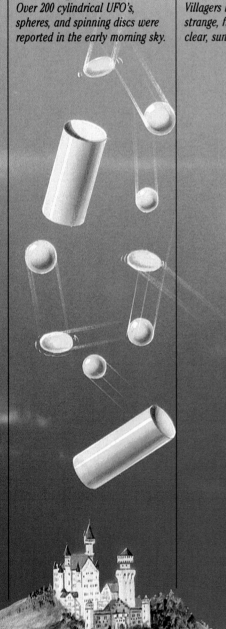

April 1561
Nuremberg, Germany
Over 200 cylindrical UFO's, spheres, and spinning discs were reported in the early morning sky.

August 1666
Robozero, Russia
Villagers leaving church told of a strange, fiery ball of light in a clear, sunny sky.

August 1883
Zacatecas, Mexico
Over 400 cigar-shaped and disc-shaped objects were reported moving across the sun.

ANCIENT ASTRONAUTS

Did alien astronauts visit our planet in ancient times? This was a firm belief in some civilizations and was reflected in their folklore and artifacts. More recently this idea has undergone a popular revival.

Ancient headgear
This prehistoric pictograph found in the caves above Capo di Ponte, northern Italy, has caused much discussion. Däniken has interpreted the dome-shaped headgear as a space helmet. Archeologists believe it is more likely that this is a crude representation of a headdress or a basket carried on the head.

Visitors from space?
Sand paintings by the Dogon people of Mali in West Africa reflect their conviction that they were visited in ancient times by extraterrestrial teachers.

THE KNOWLEDGE OF THE DOGON

The Dogon claim that alien beings came to earth from the star Sirius many thousands of years ago. The Dogon have no modern astronomical equipment, but possess a detailed knowledge of astronomy. They say they learned this from the aliens.

Star knowledge

For example, for centuries the Dogon have been able to locate the star Sirius in the night sky. They also claim that it is orbited by two planets not visible to the naked eye. The existence of one of these planets was established in the mid-19th century. If the other one is discovered, it will be impressive evidence of the truth of the Dogon's myths.

Another explanation for the Dogon's beliefs is that in ancient times they assimilated astronomical lore from the Egyptians and Babylonians. Alternatively they may have learned of Sirius from travelers or early missionaries. Whatever the real solution, the sophisticated astronomical knowledge of this African tribe leaves many questions unanswered.

F ASTRONAUTS FROM OTHER PLANETS did visit earth in spaceships in ancient times, it could explain some profound mysteries. For example, they could have brought with them the sophisticated technology that would explain how primitive societies could have achieved their extraordinary feats of construction. Anthropologists have often marveled at how buildings such as the Egyptian and Mayan pyramids were constructed, and the idea of otherworldly assistance may offer a solution.

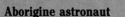

8th century B.C. Babylonian carving

Godlike architects

This was the theory that Swiss writer Erich von Däniken put forward in his book *Chariots of the Gods?* published in 1968. Although a popular bestseller, Däniken's book was met with scorn by the scientific establishment.

But Däniken's hypothesis is not an isolated theory. There are several cultures that believe in visitation by ancient astronauts. According to the cosmology of the Australian aborigines, the Wondjina spirits who created the planet descended from other worlds in flying craft. The Dogon tribe of Mali, West Africa, believe that visitors from the star Sirius descended among them and taught them the sophisticated astronomical lore that forms an important part of their tribal knowledge.

Aborigine astronaut
Australian aborigines believe that the world was created by spirits called the Wondjina who visited the earth in flying craft. When the Wondjina had accomplished their part in creation, they left behind their image painted on the walls of caves and the bark of trees.

Mayan astronaut?
Däniken interpreted the design on a Mayan tomb lid as an ancient astronaut in a spacecraft. This illustration gives some idea of what such a craft might look like.

CHARIOTS OF THE GODS?

In 1968 Erich von Däniken published his bestselling book *Chariots of the Gods?* in which he argued that beings from other planets visited our world in ancient times. Tens of millions of people have read the book worldwide, and it has been translated into 26 languages. Even though Däniken's theory provoked immediate derision from the scientific and archeological communities, his ideas had enormous popular appeal.

The mysterious sarcophagus

One of the pieces of evidence Däniken produced to support his theory was a novel interpretation of the design on an ancient Mayan tomb lid. This was excavated in 1949 by the Mexican archeologist Alberto Ruz Lhuillier in the ancient Mayan city of Palenque in what is now the Mexican state of Chiapas. It lay hidden 69 feet within the limestone pyramid known as the Temple of Inscriptions.

The carved relief decoration on the lid of the tomb certainly lends itself to different interpretations. Däniken believed that it shows an astronaut in a space capsule, working the controls with his hands. There is a pedal under his foot, and close to his face hangs some breathing apparatus, while behind him streams rocket exhaust. Other authorities suggest that there is nothing extraordinary about the carving when viewed in the context of Mayan religious art.

Nazca spacemen
Ancient rock paintings from the Nazca Plains, Peru.

Out of Uzbekistan
A mysterious image in a 3,000-year-old cave painting from Navoy, Uzbekistan, Central Asia.

Visitors from other planets?

These two ancient rock paintings were cited by Däniken as evidence for his "ancient astronaut" theory. In the Uzbekistan cave painting the humanoid figures look as if they might be wearing respirators and the object in the center may represent a spacecraft. This painting is typical of the nomadic Luristan people of southern Russia in the period from 1500 to 500 B.C. The figures with unusual helmets in the Nazca cave painting may form part of the huge patterns marked out on the Nazca plains that Däniken interpreted as a runway for ancient astronauts.

Spacecraft theory
Anthropologists interpret the Palenque tomb-lid relief as a religious tribute to the Mayan king Lord Shield Pacal. The figure's hands form part of the classic Mayan depiction of the sun. The "pedal" is in fact a seashell, which is a Mayan symbol of death. What Däniken interprets as the rocket exhaust is a symbol for the corn plant.

imagery employed. But Ezekiel's experience is not unlike that reported by later UFO contactees and abductees. He wrote of being lifted aboard a strange craft by a spirit force, and then being carried away to another world.

The Romans of more recent antiquity also recorded sightings of unexplained objects in the sky. The Roman writers Livy and Pliny each report a mysterious fiery object falling toward the earth, in 214 B.C. and 66 B.C. respectively. Julius Obsequens, who was writing in the fourth century A.D., speaks of witnesses who had seen several round shields and burning globes both by day and night in the skies above or near Rome. Medieval chroniclers echo these reports. A famous

Son of the sun
This miniature from the Mahabharata *shows the conflict between Arjuna and Karna. Karna, like his father, the sun, had only one wheel on his airborne chariot.*

machines called *vimanas*. Another ancient Indian manuscript, dealing mostly with matters of town planning and architecture, gives matter-of-fact instructions for the manufacture of various *vimanas*, although the precise meaning of specific steps and materials, and of certain alchemical formulas, remains ambiguous. The *vimanas* were claimed to have the destructive potential of today's nuclear weapons, and the leveling of the city of Varanasi (Benares) is described in detail.

In Genesis 19:24—28 brimstone and fire rained out of the heavens to cause the utter destruction of Sodom and Gomorrah. Equally striking is the strange spectacle of a fiery cloud recorded by the prophet Ezekiel around 600 B.C. Various interpretations of this event have been offered over the years, two rarely alike because of the obscure

The skies were filled with cylindrical UFO's, from which emerged black, red, and orange globes.

woodcut by Hans Glaser shows a spectacular display (likened to a war waged in the heavens) above Nuremberg, Germany, on April 14, 1561. During the early morning hours, the skies were filled with cylindrical UFO's, from which emerged numerous black, red, and orange globes or smoking spheres. A similar event, also captured in woodcut, is said to have taken place above Basel, Switzerland, on August 7, 1577. This time large numbers of black spheres appeared engaged in a furious battle.

What were our ancestors seeing? Like the biblical prophets, people in the Middle Ages tended to interpret these aerial displays as religious portents. The possibility always remains, of course, that they were simply misinterpreting ordinary atmospheric phenomena such as meteors and the aurora borealis, or northern lights. The possibility also exists that they were witnessing something truly anomalous. And as we shall see, strikingly similar sights have been reported by more modern observers as well.

Beginning in the autumn of 1896, Californians in San Francisco,

God of the sun
Helios, the Greek sun god, is depicted on this vase. Each dawn he would rise from the sea and drive his chariot across the sky.

Medieval UFO's
Strange objects were sighted in the sky over Nuremberg, Germany, on April 14, 1561. This print is from a woodcut that recorded the momentous event.

UFO's in the Bible

Many episodes in the New and Old Testaments of the Bible have been interpreted by some ufologists as evidence that alien astronauts did visit our planet in ancient times. Often these stories bear a startling similarity to modern-day reports of UFO sightings, alien contact, or abductions.

A 12th-century representation of Eli'jah being taken up to heaven.

God's creatures

The vision of the prophet Ezekiel has many of the characteristics of a close encounter with an alien spacecraft and its occupants.

As I looked, behold, a stormy wind came out of the north, and a great cloud, with brightness round about it, and fire flashing forth continually, and in the midst of the fire, as it were gleaming bronze. And from the midst of it came the likeness of four living creatures. And this was their appearance: they had the form of men, but each had four faces, and each of them had four wings. Their legs were straight, and the soles of their feet were like the sole of a calf's foot; and they sparkled like burnished bronze.

Ezekiel 1:4–7

A star in the east

The star seen in the sky when the infant Jesus was born behaved like many other UFO's before and since.

...And lo, the star which they had seen in the East went before them, till it came to rest over the place where the child was. When they saw the star, they rejoiced exceedingly with great joy....

Matthew 2:9–10

Wheels of fire

The prophet Eli'jah wrote of being transported up into heaven in a burning chariot.

...Eli'jah said to Eli'sha, "Ask what I shall do for you, before I am taken from you." And Eli'sha said, "I pray you, let me inherit a double share of your spirit."...And as they still went on and talked, behold a chariot of fire and horses of fire separated the two of them. And Eli'jah went up by a whirlwind into heaven. And Eli'sha saw it and he cried, "My father, my father!"...And he saw him no more.

2 Kings 2:9–12

Ufological exodus

Some ufologists claim that when the people of Israel were led out of Egypt by Moses they were guided on their journey by benevolent UFO's that hindered all attempts at pursuit by the Egyptian forces.

Then the angel of God who went before the host of Israel moved and went behind them; and the pillar of cloud moved from before them and stood behind them, coming between the host of Egypt and the host of Israel....And in the morning watch the Lord in the pillar of fire and of cloud looked down upon the host of the Egyptians, and discomfited the host of the Egyptians, clogging their chariot wheels so that they drove heavily....

Exodus 14:19–20; 24–25

Biblical starseed

Some believe that there is biblical evidence that visitors from other worlds bred with earthlings to begin the human race.

When men began to multiply on the face of the ground, and daughters were born to them, the sons of God saw the daughters of men were fair, and they took to wife such of them as they chose....The Nephilim [the men of gigantic stature] were on the earth in those days, and also afterward, when the sons of God came in to the daughters of men, and they bore children to them. These were the mighty men that were of old, the men of renown.

Genesis 6:1–4

Unidentified scroll

This passage describes an ancient sighting of a cylindrical UFO.

And he said to me, "What do you see?" I answered, "I see a flying scroll; its length is twenty cubits, and its breadth ten cubits."

Zechariah 5:1–2

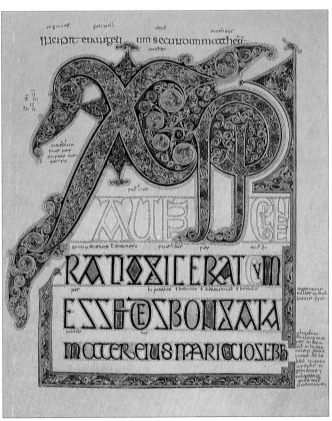

St. Matthew's Gospel
Illuminated Latin manuscript from the 7th-century Lindisfarne Gospels.

German Zeppelin
The "Great Airship" sighted over California in 1896 had many of the characteristics of the German Zeppelin airship. The Zeppelin prototype did not take to the air until July 1900 — four years after the California sightings.

Landing sites
Flat-topped mesas in Monument Valley, Utah, are now part of the Navajo Indian reservation. These natural stone monuments are reputed in Navajo myth to be sacred places where the ancient gods first came to earth.

Oakland, and Sacramento claimed hundreds of sightings of what soon became known as the Great Airship. By the following spring reports were more numerous and widespread.

Time and time again, witnesses told tales of a large cigar-shaped object moving slowly through the night skies. Some saw huge membranes like the wings of a giant insect, lighted portholes, and obscure shadows that moved about the superstructure. Others reported the chugging sound of motors, and a brilliant ray that beamed downward. It was sometimes encountered on the ground, usually in some sort of difficulty, and manned by a foreign crew. So persistent were such reports that the father of the light bulb, Thomas Alva Edison, felt compelled to call a press conference to deny that he had invented the Great Airship.

The age of aviation
In early May 1897, the sightings stopped. Skeptics claim the entire episode was nothing more than a magnificent hoax, engineered by bored railroad telegraphers and sensationalized by the popular press. Others regard the Great Airship as a precursor, physical or psychological, of things to come.

Edison called a conference to deny that he had invented the Great Airship.

A few years later, in 1903, the Wright brothers lifted a heavier-than-air contraption off the sand dunes at Kitty Hawk, North Carolina, and overnight the world entered a new age. Now we too could soar with the birds, perhaps in time as far as the sun and the other stars. But for the moment our anonymous aerial visitors remained one step ahead.

A cigar-shaped craft
In 1909 the Airship was back, this time over England, and with a more modern, faster design. The case reported by police constable Kettle of Peterborough, near Cambridge, is typical. In the early morning hours of March 23, 1909, his attention was drawn to the "steady buzz of a high-powered engine." Kettle next spied "a powerful light," which he estimated "to have been some 1,200 feet above the ground." He also saw a "dark body, oblong and narrow in shape, outlined against the stars...it was traveling at a tremendous pace, and as I

watched, the rattle of the engines gradually grew fainter."

There were hundreds of reports of a whirring sound from above, a cigar-shaped craft, and a brilliant light beaming groundward. What is apparent is that there were not nearly enough real airships in the world to explain all these sightings. The Germans, for example, had only three Zeppelins operational at the time. But up to and even after the outbreak of hostilities in 1914, northern Europe would be plagued by such reports. The Danes blamed the British, who suspected the Germans, who in turn accused the British. But the

---

"A dark body, oblong and narrow in shape, outlined against the stars."

---

mysterious craft did not cause any trouble — they seemed to be passive observers of the turmoil below.

The period between the World Wars was not without incident either. From 1933 until 1938, Norway, Sweden, and Finland were inundated with reports of the "Ghost-flier." Unlike its predecessors, the Ghost-flier was reported as a large airplane, with ordinary wings, nose, and tail. This phantom plane seemed to perform the then impossible feat of flying low over mountain terrain in snow and fog. Its arrival was often announced by a brilliant beam of light.

Foo fighters
Public apprehension was so aroused by press reports that systematic expeditions were organized in search of the Russian or German "spy bases" suspected of harboring the mysterious plane. Nothing was found, but two army planes crashed among the fjords, and one navy cruiser ran aground in the search. Less than a year later, Hitler's Blitzkrieg overran Poland. Suddenly, there was a new, totally terrestrial ogre to contend with, more malignant than any visitor from the planet Mars. But even the ensuing worldwide conflict could not conceal the fact that UFO's were being reported in the night skies. The latest UFO manifestation quickly became known as "foo fighters." The origin of the phrase itself remains uncertain, but it seems to have come from a cartoon fireman, *Smokey Stover*, popular among GI's. One of his catchphrases was: "Where's there's foo, there's fire!" ("Foo" was probably a corruption of the French word for fire, *feu*, with additional overtones of *fou*, meaning crazy.)

Foo fighters were usually reported as small luminous balls of various-colored lights, predominantly orange, green, and white. They appeared both at night and in the daytime, and were reported as playing tag with Allied fighters and bombers in both the Pacific and European theaters of operations.

Ghost rockets
The sightings of unknown aerial objects did not cease with the end of the war. No sooner had the mushroom clouds over Hiroshima and Nagasaki evaporated than Sweden began reporting strange "ghost rockets." These objects resembled the V-1 ramjet pilotless aircraft and V-2 rockets that had rained death and destruction on wartime London.

Despite the fact that the ghost rockets were photographed on several occasions and more than a thousand cases in all were cataloged, there was no satisfactory explanation. And, after a brief spate of convincing reports, the ghost rockets, like the other UFO's sighted through the ages, were seen no more in that form.

Orson Welles

WELLS OF FEAR
On October 30, 1938, Orson Welles and the Mercury Theatre troupe broadcast a realistic version of H. G. Wells's *The War of the Worlds* on CBS radio. The story tells of earth's invasion by warlike Martians, and its impact on the general public was considerable. People on America's eastern seaboard fled into the streets in terror, believing that Trenton, New Jersey, had been laid waste by extraterrestrial invaders. Shotguns were taken out of closets and loaded in preparation for the final, decisive stand against the aliens.

Newspaper reports
The cold light of morning brought abject apologies from Welles and sheepish admissions of panic from among his listeners.

Psychologists and ufologists have argued ever since: Would official admission of the presence of extraterrestrial visitors cause another mass panic? And is this why the authorities take such a skeptical view of the UFO phenomenon?

War of the Worlds
This scene from a movie of H. G. Wells's science fiction novel shows the panic in the streets as the Martians invade.

UFO's in Literature

From earliest recorded time, writers have documented for posterity many inexplicable marvels that have been witnessed in the sky. Many of the phenomena that have puzzled, amazed, and even terrified our forebears would today be described as UFO sightings. Sometimes these UFO's have become part of a culture's history and have even found their way into its legend.

Disc of destruction

"...Varanasi burned, with all its princes and their followers, its inhabitants, horses, elephants, treasuries and granaries, houses, palaces, and markets. The whole of a city that was inaccessible to the gods was thus wrapped in flames by the discus of Hari, and was totally destroyed. The discus, then, with unmitigated wrath, and blazing fiercely...returned to the hand of Vishnu."

Mahabharata (*c.* 400 B.C.)

Roman candle

"In 66 B.C. in the consulship of Gnaeus Octavius and Gaius Scribonius a spark was seen to fall from a star and increase in size as it approached the earth, and after becoming as large as the moon it diffused a sort of cloudy daylight, and then returning to the sky changed into a torch; this is the only record of this occurring. It was seen by the proconsul, Silenus, and his suite."

Pliny, *De rerum natura*, Book II (*c.* A.D. 100)

Abducted maiden

"The unseen dwellers of the woodlands watched this sad and shameful deed as the all-powerful Rasksha abducted the poor and helpless dame. He set her upon his winged chariot which shone as bright as gold, and moved as fleet as the god Indra's heavenly steed!...Then the chariot rose in the skies, high over the hill and wooded vale."

Ramayana (*c.* 300 B.C.)

Triple UFO

Edward: Dazzle mine eyes,
or do I see three suns?
Richard: Three glorious suns,
each a perfect sun,
Not separated with the
racking clouds,
But sever'd in a pale clear-
shining sky.
See, see! They join, embrace
and seem to kiss,
As if they vowed some
league inviolable:
Now are they one lamp, one
light, one sun,
In this the heaven figures
some event.

Shakespeare, *King Henry VI, Part III* (*c.* 1590)

Flying shields

"Now when the Saxons perceived things were not going in their favor, they began to erect scaffolding from which they could bravely storm the castle. But God is good as well as just....Those watching outside in that place, of whom many still live to this very day, say they beheld the likeness of two large shields reddish in colour in motion above the church, and when the pagans who were outside saw this sign, they were at once thrown into confusion and, terrified with great fear, they began to flee from the castle."

Annales Laurissenses (A.D. 900)

Circles of fire

"The scribes of the House of Life found a circle of fire that was coming in the sky...it had no head, and the breath of its mouth had a foul odor. Its body was 5 yards long and 5 yards wide. It had no voice. Now after some days had passed, these things became more numerous in the sky than ever. They shone more in the sky than the brightness of the heavens, and extended to the limits of the four supports of the heavens."

The Annals of Thutmose III
(*c.* 1450 B.C.)

Persian flying machine
This 15th-century miniature has been presented as evidence of an ancient belief in flying machines.

Riding high

"But Phaethon, in the pride of his youth and strength, leaped into the light chariot, delighted to hold the reins his father gave him....The winged horses of the sun hurled themselves forward, and, galloping into the air, tore through the clouds that hampered their way. Soaring on winged feet, they sped past the East winds....But the sun's horses felt that their burden was too light. They did not recognize the chariot which they drew....Just as curved ships toss about, if they are not carrying a full cargo, and ride the waves unsteadily, because they are not heavy enough, so this chariot, lacking its normal load, leaped into the air, and was thrown about on high, as if it were empty.

"As soon as the horses felt this happen, they raced away out of the well-beaten track, and galloped off, no longer on their usual course....[The reins] fell from his hands, and lay loose on the horses' backs. At once, the team galloped away, out of their course. With none to restrain them, they sped through regions of air unknown....They dashed against the stars set in the highest heaven....The earth caught fire, starting with the highest parts...."

Ovid, *Metamorphoses*,
Book II (A.D. 8)

Hindu spacecraft

"When morning dawned, the god Rama, taking the celestial car...stood ready to depart. Self-propelled was the car....It was large and finely painted. It had two stories and many chambers with windows....It gave forth a melodious sound as it coursed along its airy way."

Ramayana (*c.* 300 B.C.)

THE SAUCER AGE

A chance phrase from an eager reporter, and the flying saucer age was launched. Suddenly, most UFO's that came close enough to be identified as spacecraft were reported as having that distinctive shape.

N THE SUMMER OF 1947, Kenneth Arnold was the man who concentrated public attention on UFO's. A trained pilot and an apparently reliable witness, he reported seeing nine silvery, circular objects flying at a speed he calculated as over 1,200 m.p.h. above the Cascade Range, Washington state. Arnold retold his story so many times that some inconsistencies crept into the record. But whatever discrepancies were unwittingly introduced by Arnold, his experience still remains the prototypical UFO sighting, and what he says he saw continues to defy ready explanation.

No longer alone

The Arnold sighting unleashed a flood tide of similar reports. Suddenly a previously inexpressible idea was spoken aloud: humankind was not alone in the universe. Previous sightings of inexplicable objects in the sky had been interpreted either in the context of religious visions or misidentified natural phenomena, brought on by a combination of individual and social anxieties. But after Arnold's "flying saucer" sighting, a small but growing percentage of the population began to believe in the physical reality of nuts-and-bolts craft from other planets visiting the earth. UFO's were finally here to stay.

American military authorities were forced to respond to the mounting ground swell of UFO reports. On January 22, 1948, Project Sign was set up, operating under the auspices of the Intelligence Division of the U.S. Air Force's Air Matériel Command headquarters at Wright-Patterson Air Force Base, Dayton, Ohio. In February 1949 the name was changed to Project Grudge, and in March 1952, to Project Blue Book. The project was finally phased out in December 1969.

Given that UFO's appeared to be a form of advanced technology, the obvious fact that they might be crewed by intelligent beings should not have come as a shock. Still, it was one thing to see a saucer in the sky at a great distance, quite another to claim to have

Kenneth Arnold

UFO photographs
After Arnold's 1947 flying saucer report, many more sightings were claimed — and photographs were produced.

The COMING of the SAUCERS

By Kenneth Arnold & Ray Palmer

UFO books
Arnold's 1947 saucer report opened up a whole new area for books and magazines to explore.

FATE MAGAZINE
March 1955 35¢

TRUE STORIES OF THE STRANGE AND THE UNKNOWN

SAUCER OVER ITALY

Religion and the Saucer!

Fate magazine, March 1955

The Book Everyone Is Talking About
BEHIND THE FLYING SAUCERS
Frank Scully

One of the first UFO books, 1950

encountered its living occupants face to face. Soon such tales would become quite common. One of the first people to claim contact with alien beings was a Polish immigrant to the United States named George Adamski. In 1953 Adamski wrote of his encounters with the alien Orthon from the planet Venus in *Flying Saucers Have Landed,* which was an immediate bestseller. By 1959 Adamski had developed enough of a following to embark on a world tour.

A global phenomenon

A wave of UFO sightings swept America in the summer of 1947. Between June and July of that year 850 UFO's were reported to the authorities.

UFO sightings were not confined to the U.S.A. By the 1950's UFO's were patently a global phenomenon. Numerous UFO sightings were reported in France in the early 1950's. On October 27, 1952, in the town of Gaillac in southwestern France, 100 witnesses reported a cigar-shaped UFO, almost identical to a UFO that had been reported ten days earlier in Oloron, a town 130 miles due west of Gaillac.

Typical of the thousands of cases during this time is one that occurred in the early hours of August 23, 1954. Shortly after midnight, as French business-man Bernard Miserey pulled into the garage of his home in Vernon, about 40 miles northwest of Paris, he claimed to notice that his village seemed bathed in a pale light. He looked up and saw a giant, cigar-shaped object hovering silently in the sky above him, giving off a luminous glow.

In Miserey's own words: "I had been watching this amazing spectacle for a couple of minutes, when suddenly from the bottom of the cigar came an object like a horizontal disc, which dropped at first in free fall, then slowed, and suddenly swayed and dived

horizontally across the river toward me. For a very short time I could see the disc full-face; it was surrounded by a halo of brilliant light."

The disc passed overhead and disappeared at high speed into the southwest. Then "A similar object came from the cigar and went through the same maneuvers. A third object came, then a fourth." Finally, after a long interval, "A fifth disc detached itself from the cigar, which was still motionless." This last disc swooped lower than the previous four, and Miserey "could see very clearly its circular form and its red luminosity — more intense at the center, fading out at the edges — and the glowing halo surrounding it."

After pausing for a few seconds, "It wobbled like the first four, and took off like a flash toward the north, where it was lost in the distance as it gained

"The disc was surrounded by a halo of brilliant light."

altitude. During this time the luminosity of the cigar had faded, and the gigantic object, which may have been 300 feet long, had sunk into darkness. The spectacle had lasted about three-quarters of an hour."

During the next two decades significant UFO reports would come not only from Europe, but from countries all over the world, including South America, China, and Australia.

Effects on humans

Some accounts suggested that UFO's appeared capable of not just interacting with the physical environment but of affecting their human observers as well. Two well-respected French ufologists, Aimé Michel and Jacques Vallée, both gave independent accounts of just such a UFO encounter that took place in southeastern France.

At 4:00 A.M. on the morning of November 2, 1968, a French physician, known to the public only as "Dr. X," stepped out onto the balcony of his country villa to investigate a series of lightning-like flashes. According to the doctor, two identical discs were hovering about 700 feet away, each some 200 feet

SAUCER STATISTICS

A complete set of UFO statistics is difficult to compile. This is partly because of military secrecy, and partly because orthodox science has tended to shy away from the subject. From 1947 to 1969, the U.S. Air Force's investigation into the matter amassed more than 13,000 cases in its files. After astronomical bodies, man-made objects, and hoaxes were eliminated, 5 percent persisted as "unidentified."

The biggest mystery of all?

Many ufologists consider this ratio to be conservative, arguing that at least one of every ten UFO's reported defies mundane explanation. Moreover, some studies claim that only one of every 20 UFO's sighted is ever reported to the police or other authorities. A 1978 Gallup Poll revealed that 51 percent of the adult American population answered Yes when asked: "Do you think there are people somewhat like ourselves living on other planets in the universe, or not?" Only 33 percent answered No. And an amazing 57 percent thought that UFO's were real and not imaginary.

A million flying saucers

In America, one in every 11 adults, or some 23 million people, claim to have seen what they believe to be a UFO. Even if only 5 percent of UFO reports represent something anomalous, that would still leave over a million "unidentifieds" reported from the U.S.A. alone. This suggests that tens of millions of anomalous objects may have been sighted worldwide over the last four decades.

Some ufologists use these same figures to argue against the existence of alien visitors. They suggest that, in order to produce such a staggering number of experiences, something natural and/or psychological must be at the root of the phenomenon.

French flying saucers
Apart from the U.S.A. and Britain, France is the next country most affected by UFO's. It also seems to have more than its fair share of unusual cases. This has led to a considerable body of literature on the subject, from comics to more serious investigations into this strange phenomenon.

40% aircraft	35% stars and planets	10% meteors	10% others (birds, flares, hoaxes, etc.)	5% "unidentified"

wide and 50 feet thick, each with a tall vertical antenna on top. Sparks intermittently shot between the two discs, and a beam of white light struck the ground below. The two "saucers" then merged into one. At that point the doctor was hit directly by the light beam and heard a loud bang. Immediately, the single disc vanished in a spectacular shower of colorful sparks.

Two and a half weeks later, he said, a triangular-shaped patch of discolored skin, with six-inch sides, appeared around his navel. The curious triangle was said to appear and disappear annually, and photographs purporting to show it were taken.

"Miracle" cures

Even more enigmatic were the miraculous healings Dr. X claimed. Ten years earlier, he had been seriously wounded on the right side of his body in a wartime mine explosion. This injury had never healed entirely. More recently, three days before the UFO sightings, Dr. X had severed an artery with an ax while chopping wood. This wound was infected at the time of his encounter. Dr. X reported that both injuries began to heal without further treatment in the weeks after he had been blasted by the white light from the UFO.

The reported interactions between aliens and humans became closer and more intimate. The most widely publicized of these is the alleged abduction of Betty and Barney Hill. The Hills were badly shaken by the sight of a UFO while driving in the mountains of New Hampshire, and claimed to have experienced "missing time" — two and a half hours for which they could not account. Under hypnotic regression, Betty Hill told a strange story of abduction by diminutive beings, including an uncomfortable physical examination that involved the taking of skin samples and the insertion of a needle near her navel.

Less well-known is the reported abduction of police officer Herbert Schirmer on December 3, 1967. At about 2:30 P.M., near the intersection of Routes

Lights in the night
A "serious" French UFO magazine.

▶ PAGE 36

HEROES IN OUTER SPACE

For the last 60 years the exploits of sci-fi comic superheroes such as Buck Rogers, Flash Gordon, Captain America, and Superman against the universal forces of evil have led the imagination of millions of readers beyond the confines of this planet.

Flash Gordon

CERTAIN RECURRING SCIENCE FICTION themes have done much to shape people's ideas of what beings from other worlds might look like and how they might behave. Scientific and technological gimmickry has always been a popular theme. Early science fiction writers such as Jules Verne and H. G. Wells accurately predicted inventions such as atomic weapons, computers, and television.

Another theme explored by sci-fi writers was the concept of travel through time and space. In an early comic strip adventure Buck Rogers voyaged by spaceship to the planet Mongo to encounter Ming the Merciless. Another hero, Brick Bradford, traveled through time. In the comic strip world there were no dimensions through which heroes could not pass.

Birth of the comic book

The popular appeal of the comic book has been continuous since Harry I. Wildenberg of Connecticut put a simple idea to the test in the summer of 1934. The printing company he worked for produced the color comic strips for several East Coast newspapers. He suddenly realized that it would be simple to print a newspaper made up entirely of comic strips, and after a little experimentation he produced his first 64-page comic book. Its success was immediate, and before long the books were being sold for 10 cents a copy, each one containing up to 100 comic strip stories.

Science fiction stories quickly proved to be a very popular theme for comic books. These imaginative

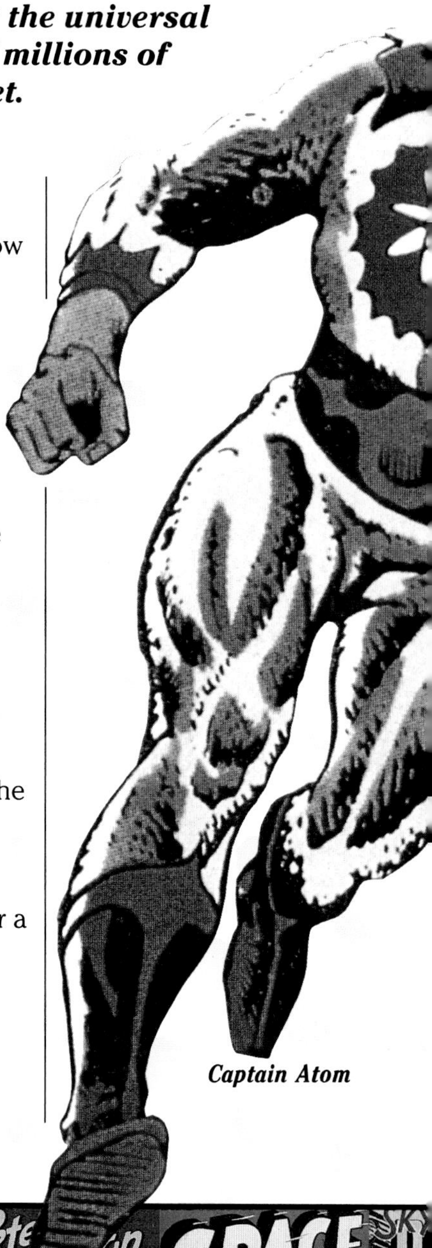

Captain Atom

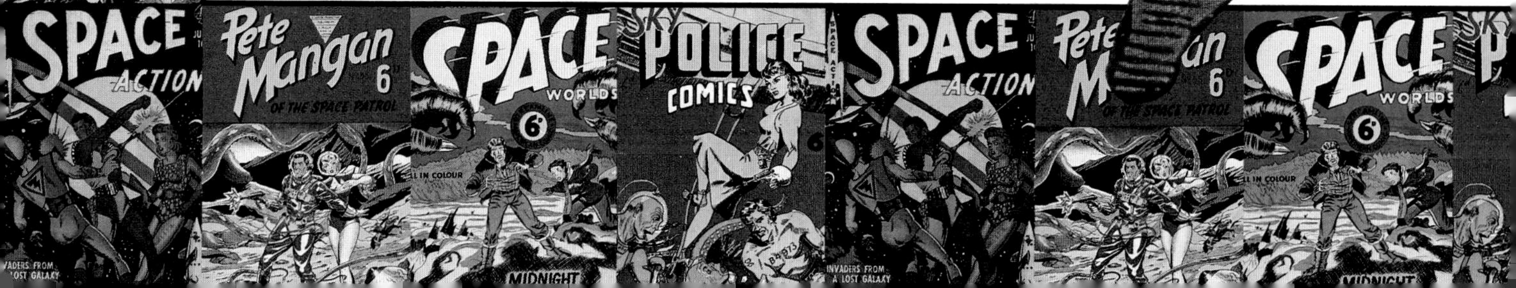

adventures almost certainly influenced the accepted idea of what distant planets and their inhabitants might actually be like.

Superheroes

One of the first sci-fi comic strip creations was Buck Rogers, a First World War flying ace who fell asleep after the hostilities ceased and awoke to find himself in the America of A.D. 2430, which has been overrun by Red Mongol hordes. He immediately embarked on a series of interstellar adventures that whetted the public's appetite for more such stories.

An early rival to Buck Rogers was Brick Bradford, who voyaged through time and space by means of a time-top that spun on its axis until it reached a planet. Brick's speciality was to overcome the machinations of evil professors who sought to dominate the various alien worlds he visited.

Scantily clad sidekicks

Close on Buck Rogers's heels came Flash Gordon, an interplanetary crusader who traveled through space by means of an atom-propelled spaceship. His helpmate on all his adventures was his girlfriend, Dale Arden, who was the first of the lovely, daring, and scantily clad

companions of the superheroes. Captain Atom was another such hero, first appearing in the 1960's. He started life as Captain Adam, a NASA scientist. Adam became Atom after being exposed to a nuclear explosion that left him with superhuman powers. For example, Captain Atom could fly through the air at speeds of more than 20,000 m.p.h. His extraordinary powers enabled him to perform exploits such as deflecting a nuclear warhead launched by aliens in an attempt to destroy earth.

Hostile aliens

For the last 60 years young men the world over — statistics have shown that 90 percent of the readers of comic books are adolescent boys — have digested the continuing exploits of Captain Atom, Captain Marvel, Brick Bradford, Flash Gordon, Buck Rogers, and Superman. The ever-inventive imaginations of science fiction writers have continued to open up a universe teeming with aliens, distant planets, awesome spaceships, and intergalactic adventures. While so much remains unexplained about the worlds beyond our planet, people will continue to sharpen their imaginations on the adventures of heroes in outer space.

Captain Marvel

OUT THERE

Howard Blum, an investigative journalist, claims to have penetrated the veil of secrecy and skepticism that characterizes the official view of the UFO phenomenon. The U.S. government says that it closed its investigations of UFO's with Project Blue Book in 1969. But Blum maintained that the government was secretly involved in "an ongoing search for extraterrestrial life."

The Tank

In his book, *Out There*, published in 1990, Blum tells how he uncovered the existence of a "UFO working group" that was meeting in a bunker known as the Tank, deep within the Pentagon.

According to Blum, the group was set up in 1987 after an unknown object flew across U.S. air space, accelerating in a way that would be technically impossible for an earthly craft. The object's flight was monitored at the air force's listening station on Cheyenne Mountain, near Colorado Springs. It was not one of the thousands of items that are known to be floating in space and that are constantly monitored. The scientists were baffled, some high-ranking air force officers were worried — and the UFO working group was born.

Regular meetings

Officially, no such group existed. Privately, however, highly placed individuals who refused to be named, assured Blum that the UFO working group was meeting regularly. The questions remain: If the official view is correct, and none of the UFO's are alien spacecraft, why is the government spending taxpayers' money on a UFO working group? And why is it so concerned to keep its findings secret?

In the winter of 1987, following a series of puzzling events, seventeen members of the U.S. intelligence community were summoned to the Pentagon. Their Top Secret mission: to determine if there was life...

OUT THERE

HOWARD BLUM

Author of *Wanted!* and *I Pledge Allegiance*

6 and 63, outside Ashland, Nebraska, Schirmer said he saw a huge, football-shaped object on the ground. It had portholes, or windows, through which red lights were flashing. Closer inspection revealed that it had a burnished aluminum skin, encircled by a catwalk, he said, and was supported on tripod legs. With a sirenlike sound, spitting reddish-orange flames, the flying football rose out of sight. Back at the station house, patrolman Schirmer nonchalantly filled out the following log entry: "Saw a FLYING SAUCER at the junction of Highways 6 and 63. Believe it or not!" The University of Colorado, under

Barney and Betty Hill

contract to the U.S. Air Force, was at that time actively investigating the UFO phenomenon. When Schirmer's sighting became known, he was briefly interviewed in Ashland, then summoned to Boulder by the Colorado University research team and examined by a psychologist, Dr. Leo Sprinkle of the University of Wyoming.

Twenty missing minutes

Schirmer spoke of an uneasy suspicion that a third of an hour of his life was missing, absent from conscious awareness, like a slate wiped clean. Following regressive hypnosis, however, strange memories and images surfaced. Schirmer related that he and his

stopped car were pulled mysteriously toward the landed object, then approached by two beings, one of whom, employing a boxlike device, "flashed *green* all around the whole car." Schirmer was, he said, suddenly lifted from his car, and asked: "Are you the watchman of this town?" And he replied: "Yes, I am."

According to Schirmer: "The crew leader had a very high forehead, and a very long nose; his eyes were sort of

"Are you the watchman of this town?"

Alien crew leader

shrunken in, and they were round eyes like ours, except for their pupils [which] were sort of the form of a...cat's eye." Schirmer added that the alien's mouth was just a slit, and that when he spoke his voice appeared to come from deep within him, and that his mouth did not move. One theory is that the alien was "talking" telepathically, a fairly common factor in reports of experiences by those claiming abduction by, or close contact with, beings from UFO's.

An ominous phenomenon

Schirmer said he was led aboard the UFO and shown its power source, which he was told worked by means of "reversible electrical-magnetism." Unlike the Hills, he was not subjected to a demeaning physical examination, nor were any blood, sperm, or skin samples taken. Schirmer said the aliens told him they were from a nearby galaxy, and that they had been observing us for a long time.

With reports of abductions, the UFO spectrum widens its horizons and assumes a more ominous aspect — if the tales are taken at face value. Some ufologists, such as Jacques Vallée, argue that abductions have always been with us, and may have nothing at all to do with extraterrrestrial

Herbert Schirmer

SIGHTING AT SOCORRO

In 1964 patrolman Lonnie Zamora said that he saw a flying saucer and its occupants in the desert in New Mexico.

Patrolman Zamora
Zamora outside the Socorro County Courthouse.

AS PATROLMAN Lonnie Zamora pursued a speeding car just outside Socorro, New Mexico, on the evening of April 24, 1964, he was, he says, startled by a roar and a burst of orange and blue flame coming from the desert. Fearing that a nearby shack used for storing dynamite might have blown up, Zamora went to investigate.

He set off cross-country in his patrol car until the terrain became too rough to proceed. As he left the car, he says, he saw a shiny white egg-shaped vehicle with a strange insignia painted in red on it. Two small, white-clad figures, each about four feet tall, stood beside it. At first Zamora thought that they were children standing by an upturned car. Zamora used his radio to call for help, reporting that he was going on foot to investigate what looked to him like a serious car crash.

Four burn marks

But as he approached it, a loud blast rent the air and, he claims, flames shot out from beneath the vehicle. Zamora took cover behind a nearby ridge and watched the craft ascend into the sky. "It appeared to go in a straight line and at [the] same height – possibly 10 to 15 feet from the ground, and it cleared the dynamite shack by about three feet...object was traveling very fast. It seemed to rise up, and take off immediately across country."

Police Sergeant Sam Chavez joined Zamora just as the vehicle disappeared. They claim that on the landing site there were four burn marks and four indentations in the stony desert ground. Later, an engineer estimated that the pressure that produced the depressions was "equivalent to a gentle settling of at least a ton on each mark." The desert shrubs were singed; one mesquite bush was still smouldering. There were small, shallow, circular indentations in the soil which could have been the footprints of the craft's occupants. Lonnie Zamora, a

sane and honest man with a policeman's eye for detail, had apparently seen a flying saucer.

Despite thorough investigations, no one has found a better explanation for what Lonnie Zamora saw in the early evening of April 24. Even the U.S. Air Force's notoriously skeptical Project Blue Book, set up to record and investigate UFO sightings, was forced to label it "unidentified."

Others were not so sure. Philip J. Klass, author of such skeptical commentaries as *UFO's: The Public Deceived, UFO's Explained,* and *UFO Abductions,* raised several objections to Zamora's account. Why didn't any of the commuters traveling on the two nearby highways see the UFO? Why didn't a couple who lived only 1,000 feet away from the site see or hear anything? Why assume that the marks on the ground had been made by alien landing gear rather than by humans? Klass concluded the sighting was a hoax designed to bring tourists to Socorro.

Inspecting the site
Zamora revisits the spot where he claims to have seen the alien spacecraft, with some researchers into the UFO phenomenon.

A reliable witness

Despite Klass's objections, the Socorro incident remains one of the most convincing UFO sightings ever recorded, because of the reliability of witness Lonnie Zamora and the traces the craft is said to have left behind. So far no one has been able to explain away the object Zamora saw or to prove conclusively that he was either in league with hoaxers, or their victim.

Spacecraft – or shovel?
Either could have caused the four mysterious indentations found at the scene of the sighting.

beings in spacecraft. Close parallels, for example, in which humans are taken away to another world and undergo transformative experiences, can be found throughout the fairy tales and folklore of almost all European countries. While Vallée believes there is a very real physical component to the phenomenon, he also thinks that UFO's may be breaking through the barriers that usually define our four-dimensional world of space and time. Before we can hope to get a grip on the problem, we may have to abandon or dramatically alter our everyday notions of reality.

A systematic genetic program

Other ufologists, such as Budd Hopkins, author of *Missing Time* and *Intruders*, view abductions as a relatively new phase of the phenomenon, as the culmination of a systematic program

UFO spotters
A large and growing percentage of the world's population now believes in the existence of nuts-and-bolts alien spacecraft. Dedicated teams of amateur UFO-watchers have spent years watching the skies in an attempt to add to the evidence.

Background UFO
As soon as UFO's became an accepted phenomenon, they began to appear everywhere. The photographer who took this shot claims he did not know it showed anything but a giraffe, until it was processed.

aimed at extracting human genetic material. From the passive observers of the past, according to this theory, the aliens have emerged as active abductors,

Abductees often appear to have entered an altered state of awareness.

interacting on a regular and covert basis with humanity. These theorists' big worry is that they feel helpless in the face of what they see as an alien invasion.

There are alternative theories. If not angels or aliens, UFO's may represent some strange hybrid of the two, an intelligence capable of interacting with human consciousness almost exclusively on its own terms, and certainly from somewhere outside the normal bounds of perception.

It may be that UFO's have more in common with poltergeists, for instance, than they do with Martians or other alien invaders. The paranormal aspects of many UFO close encounter claims are baffling. People telling of abduction often appear to have entered an altered state of awareness where the rules of everyday physics no longer apply.

Communication between abductors and humans, for example, is commonly reported as telepathic. The inside of the "spaceship" frequently appears larger than the outside, and is illuminated by a diffused, ghostly light. The reported physical examination and extraction of genetic material is often conducted in a crude, repetitious manner, as if the whole process were being staged for effect.

Myth and hallucination

Clearly, at least at this stage of our experience, the UFO-related phenomena that confront us have raised far more questions than answers. And this would still be so even if UFO's turned out to be nothing more than a mixture of myth and hallucination, an hysterical fever brought on by collective paranoia or possibly by more personal stresses and strains.

Different alien types

We would still have to ask ourselves why some UFO's reflect radar and others don't, why one light beam is said to heal while another harms. We would still want to know why some abductees report gray dwarflike beings, others tall Nordic types; why, for all their reported technological prowess in building spaceships, their science of genetic extraction and hybridization seems barely a step ahead of our own.

Why flying saucers?

We would want to know why people report flying saucers in the first place, and not, for example, green dragons, flying pigs, or pink elephants. What are we really seeing in the skies? Are UFO's merely a polished mirror reflecting our own uneasy, all-too-human dreams, aspirations, and fears? Or are they really from other planets or universes, the expression of alien dreams and intelligences?

Uninvited Flying Object
This photographer too claimed to be unaware of the UFO in the frame when he took the shot.

Speaking to the stars
The 300-yard-diameter radio telescope at the Arecibo Observatory, Puerto Rico, was first involved in the search for signs of intelligent life in space in 1960.

SETI

Many scientists believe that intelligent beings may exist elsewhere in the universe. The SETI (Search for Extraterrestrial Intelligence) program is concerned with setting up listening stations to monitor signals from about 800 nearby stars. The U.S. government has spent over $100 million on the program since 1960.

The scientists use radio astronomy to tune in to outer space. So far they have heard nothing but stellar static, the random noises of deep space.

Long-distance information

If we were to hear something, should we answer back? Some fear that alien societies with advanced technology might invade earth, once they know we are here.

But even if we don't answer, we have probably already revealed our planet's existence to interested listeners through commercial radio and television signals sent out over the past 50 years. In 1960 the first deliberate message was sent from the Arecibo Observatory in Puerto Rico to the 300,000 stars of the Messier 13 group. They are 24,000 light-years away. Even if the stars are inhabited, it will be 48,000 years or so before we get a reply.

ELVES AND ALIENS

For centuries, humankind has been entertained by wondrous stories of strange creatures: some pop out of toadstools, others descend from shining spacecraft.

A N EXPERIENCE that has apparently become quite common only recently —abduction by extraterrestrial aliens — may not be so new after all. Some of the hallmarks of the classic abduction experience have been reported for centuries. Examples are numerous: the sight of strange lights in the sky; the sudden appearance and disappearance of little people, apparently semi-human; and people who report gaps in their lives, sometimes hours, sometimes weeks, for which they cannot account in any rational way.

In the past, gnomes, dwarfs, goblins, elves, fairies, leprechauns, and bogeymen were the most common visitors from other worlds. Today they are virtually unknown, although reports of encounters with aliens from outer space are on the increase. Could it be that fairies and aliens are one and the same?

Wood carving of a gnome from southern Germany

A gnome on the earth
Gnomes are the spirits of rocks and represent the earth. Their role as guardians of the earth has been taken over today by ufonauts who exhort the humans they meet to take care of the planet and conserve its resources.

A typical alien?
Drawings of goblins bear a surprising resemblance to eyewitness accounts of a particular type of late 20th-century alien visitor. Both are small, with large heads and spindly arms and legs, and both are usually clothed in pale, close-fitting garments.

Illustration by Arthur Rackham

A 19th-century illustration of fairies abducting a child

A fairy abduction
Fairies, like modern-day aliens, were accused of using humans to improve their genetic stock. They were frequently suspected of stealing human children, and of leaving in their place sickly fairy babies, known as changelings.

Enchanted by music

Fairies often captivated humans with their music. Hapless mortals who fell under their spell returned weeks or years later thinking they had been away only a few minutes, much as today's abductees talk about periods of "missing time."

Illustration by
Arthur Rackham
from **English**
Fairy Tales

Illustration by
Florence Harrison

The bogey beast

The strange creatures that are reputed to haunt the twilight and the dark of night were often assigned a fairy origin. Nowadays, glowing eyes hovering in the darkness are more likely to be reported as UFO's or described as aliens.

Dancing lights

Although fairy stories did not put fairies in spacecraft, they were often said to float in balls of light across the twilight sky. Many places around the world are haunted by these fairy lights — also known as earth lights or spook lights — although they are now more usually reported as sightings of UFO's.

From **Margaret's**
Book *by Charles*
Robinson

An Unidentified Flying Toadstool?

Fairies live in toadstools, while aliens appear in flying saucers. Both have a similar oval shape: the gills on the underside of mushrooms resemble the propulsion systems of some UFO's.

The evil dwarf

Dwarfs were the wicked relatives of the mischievous yet charming fairies. They held sway in the depths of the earth. There is a particular type of extraterrestrial alien, usually involved in reported abductions, that is described as possessing many characteristics of the classic dwarf of folklore.

Illustration
of a dwarf
by Gordon
Wain

Stropharia
semiglobata
mushroom

CHAPTER TWO

INVESTIGATORS AND SPACECRAFT

The study of the UFO phenomenon involves a number of mainstream scientific disciplines, including physics, chemistry, astronomy, aeronautics, sociology, and psychology. Although ufology is still a fringe science, an impressive body of research has been compiled by UFO investigators since 1947.

Shortly before his death in 1986, one of the founding fathers of ufology, astronomer Dr. J. Allen Hynek, made a plea for more professionalism in the investigation of UFO phenomena. It is an unfortunate fact that anyone can form a UFO group and claim to be an expert. As a consequence, the media have given publicity to some

UFO'S AND IFO'S

The flying saucer era began in 1947 and had its heyday for the next three decades. In the period up to 1969 the U.S. Air Force collected over 13,000 reports of UFO sightings in the U.S. alone. Even the keenest UFO enthusiasts would not expect all of these to be alien spacecraft.

The proportion of sightings that can be eliminated from further study varies according to the thoroughness and bias of the researcher. But, on average, about 90 percent of all investigated reports turn out to be identified flying objects (IFO's). These are aircraft, balloons, meteors, satellites, planets, stars, unusual meteorological or light phenomena, or obvious optical illusions.

Hoaxes and fantasies

A very small percentage of reports are hoaxes, that is, deliberate attempts at fabrication. A further small percentage are fantasies: the witnesses are sincere, but the phenomena exist only in their minds. In both types of cases there is either no stimulus at all for the report, or a gross exaggeration or misperception of a minor stimulus. This does not mean that there is nothing to investigate: one of the questions raised by modern UFO research is why people have these fantasies.

Mystery sightings

The remaining 5 percent or so of UFO's do not fit into any of these categories, and resist the best efforts of analysts trained in many different fields to explain them. Despite the number of sightings, however, there is, so far, no concrete, irrefutable evidence that any of them are alien spacecraft.

dubious entrepreneurs, who seem less interested in research than in self-promotion. The two key groups in the U.S.A. are MUFON (Mutual UFO Network) and CUFOS (the J. Allen Hynek Center for UFO Studies). They both take a responsible approach and have attracted large memberships.

A belief in UFO's

Several semi-religious New Age groups have embraced ufology in peculiar ways. Not only, they say, are UFO's visiting our planet but many human beings actually originated on other worlds. It is possible to pay a fee and receive a certificate from a "psychic channel" informing you which planet you were "really" born on. A number of support groups for those who claim to have been abducted by UFO's offer counseling and therapy to help the "victims" come to terms with this disturbing experience. One enterprising company even offers an insurance policy against the possibility of individuals being abducted by extraterrestrials.

European researchers tend to be more skeptical than their North American counterparts. They tend not to accept witness reports at face value, and insist on physical evidence in order to prove the existence of alien spacecraft. In the U.S.A. the majority of researchers believe that extraterrestrial spacecraft are responsible for the unexplained UFO sightings.

There are no truly "international" UFO organizations, and until recent times little effort was put into cooperation or data exchange. Nations tend to have their own investigating groups and sets of standards, and publish magazines only in their own language.

In 1979 the British UFO Research Association (BUFORA) organized the first of a series of international

Dr. J. Allen Hynek
Hynek was director of CUFOS until his death in 1986.

conferences in London. These are held every two years in conjunction with the International Committee for UFO Research, which consists of leaders of major national groups. Other international events have been staged, for example, in Rio de Janeiro, Brazil, and Frankfurt, Germany. While these international events have attracted ufologists from all over the world, they tend to limit discussions on the origin of UFO's by taking as a starting point the assumption that extraterrestrials are visiting this planet.

Ufology remains curiously limited to Western civilization. Although there is an upsurge of interest in countries such as Russia and China, huge areas such as the Indian subcontinent have virtually no UFO organizations at all. Whether this is because there are no UFO's to study, or because the sightings are interpreted in the context of local religions or folklore, is unknown, and is a subject awaiting further research.

BUFORA in Britain has attempted to establish codes of practice for investigators in their dealings with witnesses, fellow ufologists, and the public. Other countries (notably Australia) have welcomed these new ideas, but many other nations still prefer to go their own way.

Mainstream science

In coming years, increased international cooperation and a greater tolerance of widely differing viewpoints will be essential if we are to make progress in understanding UFO's. A demonstration of ethical and scientifically responsible attitudes will also be vital to foster blossoming links between serious UFO researchers and mainstream science in many diverse fields.

THE OFFICIAL VIEW

Governments have generally been reluctant to spend money on UFO research, and few projects have made any real contribution to the debate over the origin of UFO's. The conclusions of the main official research projects are summarized here.

HE U.S. AIR FORCE operated three projects (Sign, Grudge, and Blue Book) between 1948 and 1969, of which Blue Book was the most detailed and prolonged. Over 13,000 UFO reports were studied, many received directly from military personnel. The project concluded that almost all reported UFO sightings had conventional explanations, and those that did not merely lacked the necessary data to solve them.

Project Blue Book
One of the heads of the USAF project, Major Quintanilla (seated), with his staff.

There was a small percentage of very puzzling cases, but nothing to suggest that there was any real threat to the security of the U.S.A.

The Condon Report

In March 1966 the Ad Hoc Committee to Review Project Blue Book suggested that the project be "strengthened to provide opportunity for scientific investigation of selected sightings in more detail and depth." The U.S. Air Force therefore commissioned the University of Colorado to conduct an 18-month evaluation of the UFO phenomenon.

In their official report, the Colorado scientists admitted being baffled by some of the cases, but made some interesting contributions to fields of science such as radar and atmospheric physics. However, the summary of the report prepared by the chairman, Dr. Edward U. Condon, played down the puzzling nature of a number of cases, and Project Blue Book was accordingly canceled in December 1969. The study

was fraught with controversy, and several of the scientists left to write their own more positive report recommending that UFO study be continued.

GEPAN

A French group, GEPAN, is the only team of government-funded scientists in the world established for long-term and continuous study of UFO data. In English the acronym GEPAN means "Study

---

"We must mention the preponderant role played by the psychology of perception and the subjects' interpretation of events."
(Jean-Jacques Velasco, director of GEPAN, 1987)

Group into Novel Atmospheric or Aerospatial Phenomena."

It is based at the Space Center in Toulouse, France, and employs astronomers, physicists, engineers, and legal advisers. Only cases recommended to them by the police are investigated by the scientists. Between 1977, when GEPAN was founded, and 1985, some 161 cases were studied. Then research was focused more specifically on key cases, with less public discussion of results. GEPAN scientists suspect rare atmospheric phenomena to be the cause of many UFO sightings. A very small percentage of cases still remains unexplained, but GEPAN has reached no other firm conclusions about them.

Dr. Condon and his report
Beginning in October 1966, scientists from the University of Colorado conducted an in-depth study into over 60 UFO cases. In his summary of the report, the chairman, Dr. Edward U. Condon, concluded that nothing of any scientific importance seemed likely to result from future research.

STUDY OF
UNIDENTIFIED FLYING OBJECTS
Conducted by the
University of Colorado
under contract No. 44620-67-C-0035
with the
United States Air Force
Dr. Edward U. Condon
Scientific Director
Volume 1

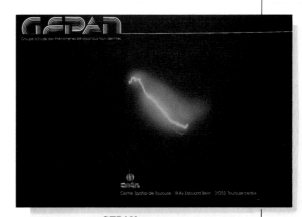

GEPAN
Promotional brochure for the French government-sponsored scientific research group into UFO's that was set up in 1977.

EVIDENCE AND TECHNIQUES

Apart from witness reports, what other evidence is there for the physical existence of alien spacecraft, and how do UFO researchers set about evaluating it?

CLOSE ENCOUNTERS of the Second Kind are defined by Dr. J. Allen Hynek in his book, *The UFO Experience*, as those in which there is tangible evidence of the appearance of a UFO. This evidence can be of the following types: physical traces, photographs, radar scans, or evidence of forces such as radiation, electricity, magnetism, or microwaves.

On August 19, 1952, "Sonny" Desvergers, a scoutmaster in his early thirties, was driving three boys from his scout troop to their homes near West Palm Beach, Florida. He spotted a flashing light, stopped the car, and set off with a machete and a flashlight to investigate. He hacked his way toward the light through the undergrowth and emerged into a clearing. There he says he was almost overwhelmed by the heat and a strange smell. He looked up, and the sky was blotted out by a huge shape above him. It hovered 30 or 40 feet above the ground, and appeared to be disc-shaped and metallic. As he shone his light at it, red light from the object engulfed him, and he passed out.

Physical traces

Desvergers had instructed the boys to go for help if he did not return soon, and they brought two policemen to the spot just in time to see him staggering out of the bushes. He appeared shocked but not

His cap was singed and his face and arms were slightly burned.

seriously hurt, though his cap was singed and his face and arms were slightly burned. In the clearing they found the machete and light he had dropped when he lost consciousness, and an indentation in the grass where he had lain.

Desvergers was subsequently interviewed by two U.S. Air Force intelligence officers. Initially believing his story, they later collected background evidence that threw some doubt on it. Physical evidence was almost entirely lacking: there were no marks at the site, and no trace of radioactivity; the machete too was tested and found to be free from magnetism and radioactivity. Only Desvergers's minor burns and singed cap

Laboratory analysis
Physical traces of alien spacecraft would be the most compelling evidence that they exist. Testing physical evidence in the laboratory, for example by checking clothing, grass, and soil found at the site for radioactivity, can give clues as to whether or not the phenomenon is unearthly.

suggested that his story might be true. Until, that is, the investigating officers sent some clumps of grass from the site to an agronomy laboratory to be examined. The roots were found to be badly charred, but the blades of grass were not affected.

Burn marks

No one could explain this satisfactorily. The charring was consistent with the ground being heated to a temperature of 300°F. The only probable way that this effect could have been produced was by a powerful alternating magnetic field inducing a current into the roots. This could also have produced sparks (which would account for the burns) and ozone (which could have been the strange smell that Desvergers reported). His lapse into unconciousness could have been caused by breathing too strong a concentration of ozone. Cases such as this are few and far between. The physical evidence is of a sort that cannot be easily faked. Despite this, in the end, the U.S. Air Force wrote the incident off as a hoax.

In most UFO cases the physical evidence is of a simpler kind. It usually consists of burn marks on the ground (allegedly caused by the spacecraft's engines) and/or indentations (said to be caused by the spacecraft's landing gear). Skeptics have no difficulty in accounting for the burn marks as the effect of lightning striking the ground, and for the indentations as a simple hoax. Although what are alleged to be fragments of crashed saucers have been found, analysis of the material has provided no real evidence that it was of extraterrestrial origin. Photography would appear to offer the best opportunity

UFO tracks?
Police examine strange markings at the site of a reported UFO landing near Richmond, Virginia, in April 1967.

I was burned by a UFO
On September 10, 1981, Denise Bishop was standing outside her home in Plymouth, England, when she spotted a large flying saucer hovering overhead. She claimed that as she stood with her hand on the door handle, a green beam of light shot out from the UFO and burned her hand. A burn was still clearly visible when this photograph was taken 36 hours after the incident.

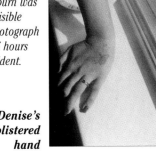

Denise's blistered hand

to demonstrate that at least some UFO's are alien spacecraft. After all, the argument goes, if alien spacecraft exist, then it must only be a matter of time before one is photographed.

Poor-quality photographs

Unfortunately nearly all the photographs of UFO's that have not been discredited are of poor quality. This is not surprising. Many UFO's appear unexpectedly, often in the far distance, and photographers do not usually have the right equipment to get a sharp image. Most UFO's are seen at night, and photographers are likely to have daylight film in their cameras.

Of course, most UFO sightings are just not photographed. As one Canadian witness put it: "If I'd been standing on a stack of cameras I'd never have thought of picking one up." An encounter with a UFO can be so awesome that witnesses forget they have a camera. Even if they remember, they may not want to risk the UFO vanishing from sight while they reach for the camera.

Nevertheless, there is evidence, in the form of both still and moving pictures — but not as much as perhaps could be expected. Although the ownership of cameras has quadrupled in the past three decades, and the ability of film and equipment to record images at night has vastly improved, the number of UFO photographs being submitted for analysis has fallen year by year. Why? Have the aliens gone home? Can they make their spaceships invisible? Is it relevant that very many early photos were fakes that attracted enormous publicity?

Advanced investigation techniques are now available using methods developed from the technology of the deep-space probes. Computers can be used to enhance images and expose fakes that once might have fooled the world. In 1962, photographs taken by a schoolboy who painted dark blobs on a sheet of glass and filmed the sky through it deceived both BUFORA (the British UFO Research Association) and the British Ministry of Defence.

Today there is no excuse for being taken in by anything but the most complex of hoaxes. This can happen only to the media so desperate for a story, or UFO groups so keen to believe, that they do not use the techniques that modern analysis can offer. The overwhelming majority of reliable

---

An encounter with a UFO can be so awesome that witnesses forget they have a camera.

---

photographs and films depict nothing more than blobs of light, glowing masses, and ill-defined shapes. They are proof that something was seen, but not acceptable evidence that this something was an alien spacecraft.

Very few photographs exist of objects that, if not fakes, clearly are structured craft. Some of these may well show experimental aviation or space prototypes that were on the secret list and hence remained unacknowledged by the government.

Radar scans

In the early days of flying saucer sightings there were several cases of a UFO being detected by radar. This happens far less often today. Radar systems were still being perfected, and many examples of strange objects shooting at high speeds across screens proved to be nothing more sinister than atmospheric echoes that were not understood then.

Today's air traffic radars usually rely on a transponder device within the aircraft. They cannot detect aircraft that do not have a functioning transponder. Aircraft may also have weather radar on board to pick out storm systems in flight. Occasionally pilots detect UFO's, but weather radar usually tracks only objects that are far bigger than a typical UFO. Radar evidence is therefore less substantial than we might expect.

Evidence of forces

Witnesses often report that UFO's generate forces of some sort. These are said to affect people and animals, electrical equipment, and the ground. In some cases the electrical forces can be measured by scientific instruments such as Geiger counters and magnetometers. There are many reports of UFO's causing severe injury to witnesses in close proximity. In December 1980, two women and a child in Huffman, Texas, suffered what appears to have been radiation poisoning. One of the women required prolonged hospitalization.

Rashes, burns, and sickness are features of many other close encounter stories. Medical investigations of the data and of some witnesses who have been hospitalized reveal that there are different types of energy involved. In a few very severe cases, witnesses are alleged to have died after over-exposure to the energy emanating from UFO's. In March 1978, a man from Cheshire, England, reported being hit by a "beam of light"; he later contracted two kinds of cancer, which claimed his life. At Salto, Uruguay, a dog died in February 1977 after approaching a spinning object that also caused electrical interference at a farm. An autopsy later revealed that the cause of death may have been exposure to radiation.

Electrical interference

There is further evidence that real forces of some kind were at work. In the Cheshire case mentioned above, a radio transceiver exploded when the lethal light beam hit the aerial. At Salto, electrical interference at the farm resulted in a generator being burnt out.

Permanent damage to machinery is rare, however. Temporary malfunction of machinery is a much more common feature, appearing in many UFO reports, usually in the form of the stalling of a car engine. This is not considered a reliable form of evidence because it tends to disappear along with the UFO itself.

Looking for clues
In the early days of UFO research, bomb-disposal squads were sometimes called in to investigate alleged UFO landing sites, using mine detectors.

The Blackbird
This SR-71 surveillance plane was first test-flown in the 1960's.

The B-2 bomber
This revolutionary aircraft had its maiden flight in July 1989.

STRANGE CRAFT

For several decades the U.S. Air Force has been pursuing a top-secret program of building "Stealth" aircraft, designed primarily to evade detection by opposing forces. In recent times there is evidence that prototypes of the SR-71 Blackbird and the Lockheed F-19, as well as the B-2 bomber, have been sighted by witnesses and classified as UFO's before their existence was officially acknowledged.

ECM equipment

Stealth planes are designed to operate quietly, often at high altitude, and some of them are notable for their outlandish shapes. This may explain why untrained civilian witnesses are not immediately able to identify them as aircraft. Their electronic countermeasures (ECM) equipment can make them invisible to radar, which may also explain why some visual sightings lacked a corresponding radar trace. The U.S. Air Force were probably happy to let such misidentifications continue, since this gave them more freedom to test-fly these aircraft. Most serious researchers treat with extreme caution any UFO's sighted near air force bases or military installations.

CROP CIRCLES

Since medieval times, perfectly regular circles of flattened crops have been mysteriously appearing in fields in the dead of night.

WIND VORTEX THEORY

British meteorologist Dr. Terence Meaden has developed a very plausible theory to explain the circles. He suggests that there exists a hitherto unrecognized atmospheric phenomenon, called the plasma vortex. Air flowing over uneven terrain becomes turbulent and forms small-scale vortices. These columns of spinning air break down explosively, causing a burst of air to hit the ground and flatten whatever crops are beneath it.

Dr. Meaden
A world authority on crop circles, and director of the Circles Effect Research Group (CERES), which gathers reports from all over the globe.

Swirling straw
The force of the vortex whirls loose debris into the air.

Glowing vision

The plasma vortex can be described as a cross between ball lightning and a tornado. Dust and pollen caught up in the whirlwind can become electrostatically charged and glow. Witnesses may mistake these lights for UFO's.

Accompanying electromagnetic fields could also stall car engines and may even be able to induce hallucinations.

This theory accounts for many of the signs of the classic UFO encounter. But it does not explain the appearance of the more complex patterns, with their slots and multiple rings.

GEORGE PEDLEY OF TULLY, North Queensland, Australia, was driving through farmland on January 19, 1966, when he saw what he thought was a spaceship rise up out of a swamp.

He later found a circular depression 30 feet in diameter in the reeds below where the object had appeared. The reeds were swirled around in a clockwise direction, as if they had been subjected to a great rotary force. Under the depression three holes were discovered; supporters of the alien spaceship explanation interpreted these as the indentations made by landing gear.

Abstract designs

The circular shape that George Pedley found is typical of the phenomenon. Crop stalks inside a circle are compressed into a tightly knit carpet, as if a great weight had descended on them.

The patterns, however, vary widely: small, simple circles are most common in the U.S.A., while in Europe the circles tend to be larger, sometimes with additional abstract designs. They vary in size from 18 inches to a massive 200 feet in diameter.

Crop circles have been found all over the globe, notably in Australia, France, Japan, and the U.S.A., but they appear most frequently in the counties of Wiltshire and Hampshire in England.

UFO landing sites?

It has been suggested that these peculiar crop circles are actually the landing sites of alien spacecraft. Many crop circle manifestations are preceded by eyewitness reports of UFO's, eerie orange lights, and strange noises. Some ufologists investigating crop circles are beginning to take this link seriously.

Since the early 1980's other researchers have been trying to isolate the force responsible for these

Abstract crop patterns

Mowing devil at work
This 17th-century English woodcut shows the diabolic agency our ancestors assumed was responsible for crop circles.

circles match the size of a helicopter's rotors, and they have been known to appear under power lines, where no helicopter could venture. Perhaps the

The overnight appearance of crop circles has been recorded since medieval times.

cause is farm machinery? The most fundamental objection to all these mechanical arguments is that the overnight appearance of crop circles has been recorded since the Middle Ages, before these machines were invented.

Differing theories

Archeologists have argued that the circles could be forming over ancient sites of human settlement; soil scientists blame chemical disorders within the soil for weakening the crop; meteorologists have even suggested that lightning could create the patterns. Another theory is that the circles are caused by rampaging hedgehogs. Swiss author Erich von Däniken believes that they are messages from outer space, and that the distinctive shape of the crop circle is a type of code, representing a molecule.

Apart from the alien spacecraft landing-site theory, the most widely supported explanation so far is that the circles are caused by wind turbulence. Other plausible theories include the effects of a fungus, and the actions of a well-orchestrated band of hoaxers.

markings. Physicists have suggested that electromagnetism may be the answer. But the force needed to charge all the plant stems within a large circle would be colossal, far beyond anything we can yet envisage on earth. Another idea is that piezoelectric forces (different levels of electrical pressure) could attract the plant stems and cause the circular arrangement. How either of these forces could produce the more complicated patterns has not been explained.

Man-made phenomena

More practical minds have suggested that man-made machinery is responsible. The downdraft from a descending helicopter would seem to be an obvious suspect. But this would not create the distinctive swirling pattern. Nor do many of the

UNDERGROUND ATTACK

The circles could be due to the action of the fungus that forms toadstool fairy rings. These can grow to over 100 feet in diameter.

The toadstool is only the fruit of the fungus, whose main growth occurs below ground. It spreads radially, attacking and feeding off the crops' roots and so causing a weakness in the stems. A light summer breeze can then make the crops collapse.

It is suggested that the circles form only at night because of the added weight of dew on the weakened stems. The swirling patterns are due to the prevailing winds; and the perfect circles are created by the fungus spreading at an equal speed in all directions. This theory can even explain the glowing lights — it is simply the phosphorescence found in fungi.

A fungus fairy ring

Saucer or scythe?

One of the most obvious explanations is that the crop circles are an elaborate practical joke. But this does not seem to be the case. A few rings have been faked, but a hoax is obvious even to the untrained eye. The circles' edges are rough, the straws are broken, and the patterns are simple.

One method of creating a hoax is to drive a stake into the ground, and attach one end of a rope to it. The hoaxers then walk around in ever-larger circles, releasing the rope little by little, their feet simply flattening the crop.

Blatant hoaxes
The precise patterns of the true circles are difficult to reproduce, as these ill-defined hoaxes demonstrate.

Dan and Grant Jaroslaw

HOAXES AND FAKES

Fewer UFO's are reported nowadays than at the start of the flying saucer era. Hoaxers know they are more likely to be exposed by the increasingly sophisticated methods of UFO investigators. The most popular form of hoax is the photograph. Some photographs are faked — by people who believe in alien spacecraft — in order to confound the skeptics. Some are faked for publicity and the money gained from selling the pictures to the media. Some are simply pranks.

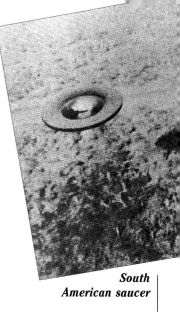
South American saucer

BROTHERLY DECEPTION

On January 10, 1967, the Jaroslaw brothers (Dan, 15, and Grant, 17) of Mount Clemens, Michigan, took four Polaroid photographs of a flying disc in their backyard. After weeks of exhaustive examination, experts could not prove that the pictures were hoaxes. For the next nine years the photographs were accepted as classic examples of a flying saucer appearing in daylight.

Fake exposed

In 1976 the eminent ufologist Dr. J. Allen Hynek received a letter from the Jaroslaws admitting the photographs were fakes. Dan, it transpired, had made a model of a flying saucer for a joke. The brothers had hung it on clear thread between two poles and photographed it. The weather conditions at the time obscured the thread. On seeing the pictures, the boys' mother contacted the newspapers, and matters moved beyond their control. "We are sorry if we caused anyone any trouble over this," concluded the letter to Hynek.

Light reflections

On July 16, 1952, in Salem, Massachusetts, Coast Guard officer Shell Alpert saw four brilliant egg-shaped objects in the sky as he looked through his office window. He rushed for his camera and snapped the lights before they vanished. At first, investigators assumed that he had faked the pictures by taking a double exposure. Later they concluded that the objects were reflections of indoor lights on the windowpane.

UFO's over Salem, Massachusetts

The Jaroslaws' faked flying disc

Brazilian flying disc

A journalist and a photographer reported seeing this flying saucer at Barra da Tijuca, on the coast of Brazil near Rio de Janeiro, in May 1952. Investigators working on the Condon Report showed the photograph to be a fake. The shadow on the disc appears on the right while the shadows of the trees and shrubs fall on the left. It appears that two separate pictures have been combined and afterwards rephotographed.

A shadowy saucer

Flying button

In 1963 a Venezuelan newspaper report claimed that an airline pilot had photographed this flying saucer during a flight over Venezuela. However, investigation revealed that the picture had been faked by an engineer in Caracas. He had placed a photograph of a button on an enlargement of an aerial shot and then rephotographed both images. The shadow beneath the so-called flying saucer, as well as the plane's shadow, were added at the printing stage.

The saucer hovers...

...banks and turns...

...and when it comes to rest an alien spaceman emerges.

A model saucer

In July 1952 an Italian engineer, Gianpiero Monguzzi, produced a series of photographs he claimed to have taken of a flying saucer in the Alps of northern Italy. After an investigation, the hoax was uncovered. The flying saucer in the mountainous terrain was a fake placed on a table-top model of the landscape. In other photographs in the sequence, the "saucer" appeared as if in flight. It was, in fact, suspended by a clear thread.

FAKING A PHOTOGRAPH

It is not difficult to fake a convincing UFO photograph, as these pictures show.

A streak of light
This UFO photograph actually shows a streetlight. The photographer moved the camera while keeping the shutter open for several seconds.

Saucer of light
This flying saucer shape is actually the reflection of a ceiling light on a pane of glass. A sheet of black paper was suspended from the ceiling, corresponding in length to the depth of the lampshade. It was hung between the shade and the windowpane, blocking out any other parts of the shade that might be reflected onto the glass.

Negative UFO
A photographic negative reverses areas of light and dark in an image. The negative of a picture of the moon was combined and reshot with a photograph of a rural scene to produce this image.

Moon as a UFO
The shining UFO in this photograph is the moon. The picture was taken with a long exposure — approximately one minute. The camera captured the moon as it traveled across the sky, creating the lozenge shape of the UFO. The picture of the night sky was then superimposed on that of a seascape, and rephotographed.

PHYSICAL FAKES

One out of 11 people in the U.S.A. is on record as having seen a UFO. Very few sightings of UFO's can be attributed conclusively to deliberate hoaxes. This is mainly because they are quite complicated to set up. However, as long as people want to believe in UFO's — and there are pranksters to fuel this belief — fakes will continue to appear in the sky.

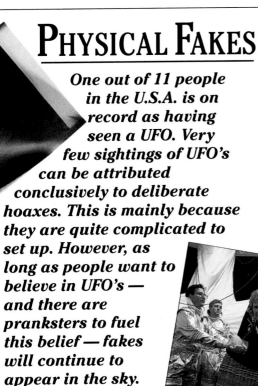

Richard Branson

The April Fool's balloon

April Fool's flying saucer

Early morning commuters driving on a freeway outside London, England, on March 30, 1989, soon after 5:00 A.M., could scarcely believe their eyes. Hovering above them was what looked like a glowing spacecraft. Oddly dressed occupants were also visible. Soon the police were inundated with calls from alarmed people.

This alien visitation proved no more sinister than British entrepreneur, and keen balloonist, Richard Branson, rehearsing a stunt for an April Fool's Day prank. The spacecraft was a saucer-shaped hot-air balloon, 100 feet wide, complete with flashing lights. The "aliens" were Branson and two co-pilots dressed as Martians.

Unobserved UFO

In December 1954, *Weird Science-Fantasy* magazine reported an experiment conducted in Ottawa by Project Magnet, the Canadian government's flying saucer investigation agency. One July night in 1954 Magnet launched an aircraft flare — the equivalent in brightness to 500,000 candles — suspended beneath a weather balloon. The flare illuminated the underside of the balloon and made it look like a flying saucer. The balloon rose to a height of 5,000 feet and passed over a stadium packed with people watching a baseball game. It also flew over two crowded drive-in movie theaters. Yet not one person reported seeing anything unusual in the sky that night. The magazine concluded that even more UFO's would be seen if people just looked up into the sky more often!

Project Magnet

The Canadian government's UFO experiment of July 1954 was reported in Weird Science-Fantasy *magazine.*

INVESTIGATING UFO's

This startling photograph of a glowing saucer flying over Manhattan looks real enough. But modern computer analysis techniques soon revealed it as a hoax.

ROUND SAUCER WATCH (GSW) is an organization that was set up in Cleveland, Ohio, in 1957 to investigate UFO sightings. A countrywide network of over 500 engineers, physicists, and astronomers, many of whom work in the aerospace industry, apply their expertise to the scientific analysis of UFO reports. In 1974 GSW began to use computers to analyze UFO photographs and proved that over 90 percent of previously accepted UFO photographs were either hoaxes or misidentifications. The techniques it developed have become standard practice in the analysis of photographs of UFO's.

Image enhancement

Using a television camera linked to a computer, GSW is able to scan a UFO photograph on the screen. The image is then broken down into 245,000 minute squares — consisting of 512 columns and 480 rows — called "pixels," or picture elements. The computer is programed to assign each of these a rating according to its brightness. These range from 0 for black to 30 for white. The pixels are then called up on a television screen to form an enhanced black-and-white image of whatever section of the photograph is being analyzed.

This technique immediately reveals whether a negative has been tampered with in any way, or whether the UFO image is the result of a blemish on the photographic emulsion, or a scratch on the negative. Studying the pixels along the edge of an image can also give a reasonably accurate measure of the object's distance from the camera.

Color contouring

GSW has also developed a technique called color contouring that links the computer to a color TV set. The human eye finds it difficult to differentiate between shades of gray, so this technique helps us read computer-enhanced images. The pixels of the photograph are coded with 32 different colors, according to brightness. The darker shades are colored red and violet. Lighter areas are assigned shades of yellow, green, and blue. The lightest areas are white.

Color contouring reveals the density of an object. For example, an uneven density of color may reveal that what appeared to be a nuts-and-bolts spacecraft is in fact a cloud. Gradually varying color density found at the edges of an image confirms that it is three-dimensional, rather than, for example, a flat image cut out and superimposed on a landscape.

Reflected light
GSW analyzed a color-contoured photograph to see how the behavior of the light emitted or reflected by the UFO compared with that from other identifiable objects in the photograph.

New York UFO
William H. Spaulding, Western Division Director of GSW, agreed to analyze this photograph of a UFO circling the Statue of Liberty in New York City. He concluded what we already knew, that it was a hoax. It is in reality a cleverly retouched photograph of a car's hubcap, superimposed on a photograph of the Manhattan skyline.

3-D enhancement
GSW highlighted the horizontal and vertical coordinates of different sections of the photograph. This creates a very sharp 3-D effect, increasing the detail, and allowing the structure of the UFO to be compared with other objects.

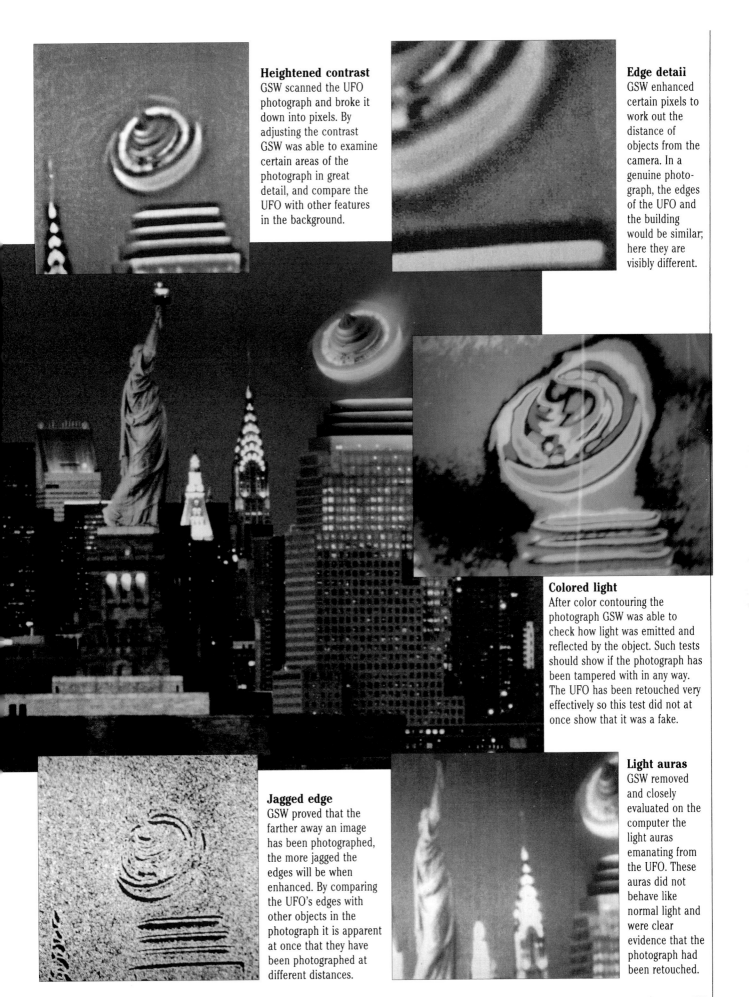

Heightened contrast
GSW scanned the UFO photograph and broke it down into pixels. By adjusting the contrast GSW was able to examine certain areas of the photograph in great detail, and compare the UFO with other features in the background.

Edge detail
GSW enhanced certain pixels to work out the distance of objects from the camera. In a genuine photograph, the edges of the UFO and the building would be similar; here they are visibly different.

Colored light
After color contouring the photograph GSW was able to check how light was emitted and reflected by the object. Such tests should show if the photograph has been tampered with in any way. The UFO has been retouched very effectively so this test did not at once show that it was a fake.

Jagged edge
GSW proved that the farther away an image has been photographed, the more jagged the edges will be when enhanced. By comparing the UFO's edges with other objects in the photograph it is apparent at once that they have been photographed at different distances.

Light auras
GSW removed and closely evaluated on the computer the light auras emanating from the UFO. These auras did not behave like normal light and were clear evidence that the photograph had been retouched.

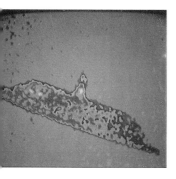

The Trent photographs

The most famous UFO photographs that GSW has analyzed are those taken by Paul Trent in McMinnville, Oregon, on the evening of May 11, 1950.

At about 7:45 P.M. Mrs. Trent was, as usual, in her farmyard feeding the rabbits. Suddenly she looked up and saw above her an enormous metal disc gliding silently through the gray evening sky. She immediately called to her husband, who was in the house. When he realized what was happening, he rushed to his car to get his camera.

The metal disc was moving rapidly through the sky as Paul Trent emerged with his camera. It looked bright and metallic, and there was no smoke or vapor coming from it. Mr. Trent quickly snapped a picture, wound the film on, and turned to follow the object as it moved across the sky. He snapped a second frame some 30 seconds later. Mrs. Trent said that the object seemed to glide before it accelerated into the west.

Mr. Trent had already used up some of the film on the roll. This proved important later when investigators studied the negatives. They compared the frames on which the UFO appeared with the rest of the film. If the negatives had been tampered with in any way, this would have been evident at once. A few days later Mr. Trent had the film developed. He told a few friends what he had seen. He intended to do nothing further. He was afraid that he might have photographed some secret government weapon.

On the cover of *Life*

Matters were taken out of his hands when a reporter on the local *McMinnville Telephone Register* heard about the photographs. The journalist pursued the story and eventually obtained the negatives. Within a week the photographs appeared on the cover of *Life* magazine and caused a sensation.

The two photographs have subsequently been scrutinized by every leading UFO expert. In 1969, after rigorous scientific examination, the skeptical scientists working on the Condon Report accepted that the object in the photographs could not be explained by any known natural or supernatural phenomena. The Condon Report concluded: "The most direct interpretation of the photographs confirms precisely what the witnesses said they saw."

GSW was able to endorse the findings of the Condon Report in 1974 when its experts analyzed the photographs using edge enhancement and color contouring. GSW found that the object was not suspended by wire, a technique used to fake many UFO photographs.

Color contouring the photograph indicated that the object was a three-dimensional shape with a flat, evenly lit underside. Comparison of the UFO image with objects in the foreground of the photograph further confirmed that it was at least half a mile away. GSW experts estimated that the object was between 60 and 90 feet in diameter. They, too, concluded that the photographs were not hoaxes.

Photograph 1
Forty years after Paul Trent took his famous photographs of a UFO, there has been no satisfactory explanation of what he actually saw. Trent's first photograph captures the UFO's unusual turreted outline. This shape is not recognizable as any man-made craft.

Photograph 2
Trent's second picture showed the disc at a different angle. No traces of any supporting wires were found when its edges were enhanced (inset).

Color contouring
The disc was shown to be a solid object with a flat underside.

YOUR OWN UFO INVESTIGATION

When investigating a UFO sighting, use the following guidelines to determine whether the case merits in-depth research.

THE ONLY WAY TO OBTAIN a reliable UFO report is to interview the witness personally. Most unidentified flying objects turn out to be sightings of natural phenomena. It is important to ascertain as soon as possible if a witness has seen something that requires further investigation.

Basic procedure

◆ Record the name, age, sex, and profession of the witness.
◆ Ask if the witness has seen a UFO before. Is the witness interested in UFO's? Does the witness have any knowledge of aeronautics?
◆ Inquire discreetly into the witness's reliability.
◆ When and where did the sighting take place?
◆ How long did the sighting last? (Anything less than 15 seconds is probably not worth investigating.)
◆ Was the location rural, urban, or industrial? Were there any military installations or airfields nearby?
◆ What was the weather like? If daytime, were any birds or planes visible? If nighttime, were there any stars visible?
◆ How many objects did the witness see? Can the witness make an accurate estimate of size?
◆ Were there any known features against which the witness could judge the size of the object?

How bright was it? Did it change color?
◆ What was the object's position and angle above the horizon when it appeared and disappeared? Was it stationary? If it moved, how fast was it and what was its trajectory? Did the object change shape or rotate?
◆ Did the witness experience any physical or psychological effects?
◆ Were any nearby animals affected? Was there any electrical interference?
◆ Were there any traces left on the ground? Measure and photograph any traces as soon as possible. Collect soil samples where relevant.

The data you collect can be analyzed to eliminate Identified Flying Objects (IFO's) such as the moon, stars, planets, aircraft, etc., from your inquiry, and to alert you to the possibility of a hoax. You may need help to analyze your data. The best way to become an effective researcher is to join a local UFO group and to pool your efforts and resources.

Size and position

Use a straight arm to estimate the object's angle above the horizon. Compare the UFO with identified objects such as the moon, a distant plane, or a house or a tree, in order to estimate its size.

UFO report
It is important to record all data promptly after a UFO sighting in order to determine whether or not it merits further investigation. UFO report forms are a valuable aid to such research. Draw up your own forms or obtain them from your local UFO group.

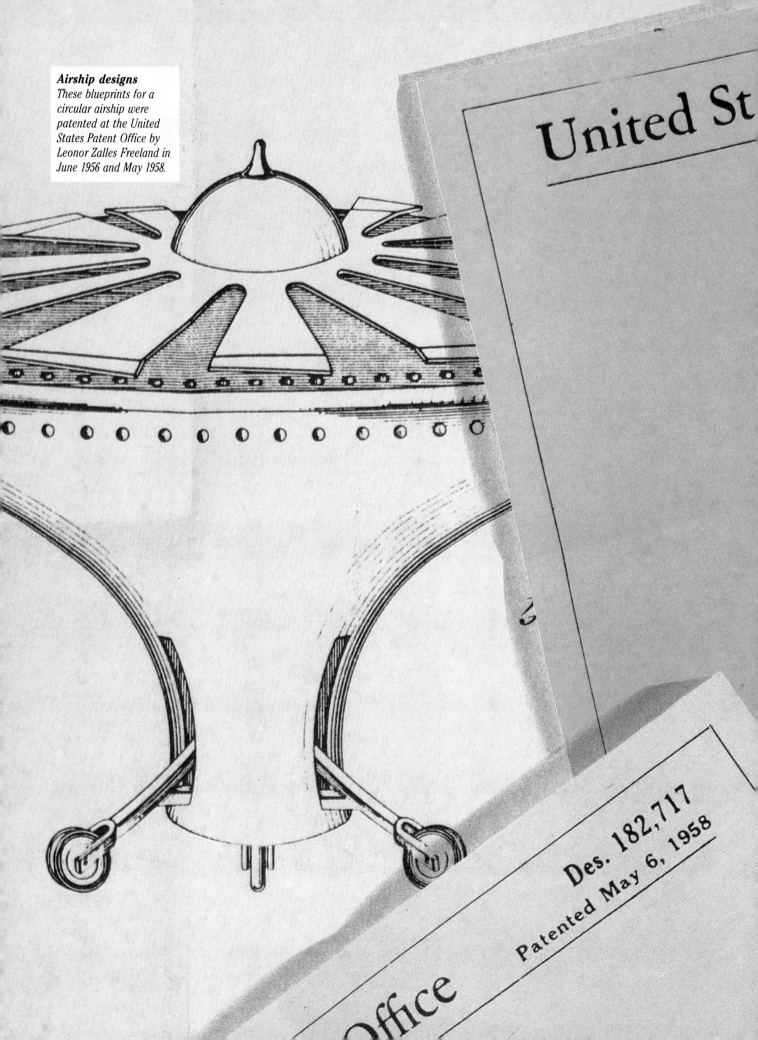

United St

Des. 182,717
Patented May 6, 1958

Office

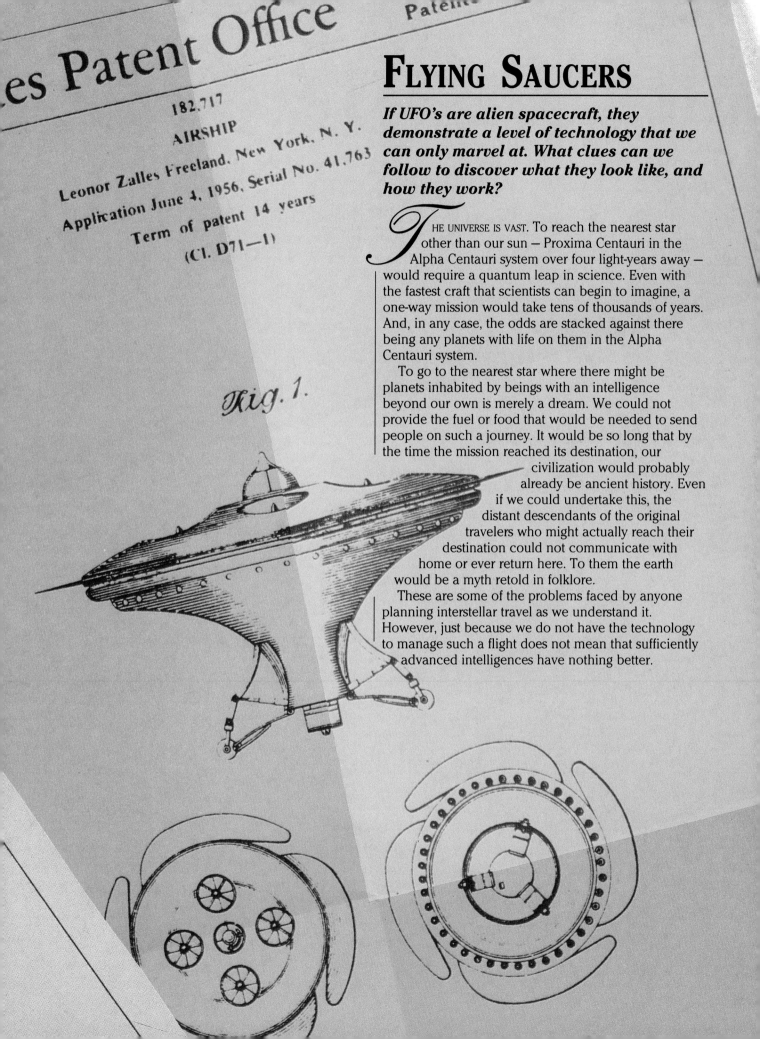

Fig. 1.

FLYING SAUCERS

If UFO's are alien spacecraft, they demonstrate a level of technology that we can only marvel at. What clues can we follow to discover what they look like, and how they work?

THE UNIVERSE IS VAST. To reach the nearest star other than our sun — Proxima Centauri in the Alpha Centauri system over four light-years away — would require a quantum leap in science. Even with the fastest craft that scientists can begin to imagine, a one-way mission would take tens of thousands of years. And, in any case, the odds are stacked against there being any planets with life on them in the Alpha Centauri system.

To go to the nearest star where there might be planets inhabited by beings with an intelligence beyond our own is merely a dream. We could not provide the fuel or food that would be needed to send people on such a journey. It would be so long that by the time the mission reached its destination, our civilization would probably already be ancient history. Even if we could undertake this, the distant descendants of the original travelers who might actually reach their destination could not communicate with home or ever return here. To them the earth would be a myth retold in folklore.

These are some of the problems faced by anyone planning interstellar travel as we understand it. However, just because we do not have the technology to manage such a flight does not mean that sufficiently advanced intelligences have nothing better.

Condon and the universe
Dr. Edward U. Condon, physicist and UFO investigator, ponders the vastness of the universe. To some, this immensity suggests the existence of other forms of intelligent life. To others, it suggests the enormous difficulties of interstellar space travel.

A UFO chart
In 1968 the Committee on Science and Astronautics of the U.S. House of Representatives studied this table of recorded UFO shapes.

And scientists talk of revolutions in our understanding of physics that might one day sweep aside these difficulties. As yet we cannot know if this is science fiction or future reality, but it does suggest that we should retain open minds about visiting other planets one day. The future will bring amazing discoveries that are unimaginable at the moment. And if we shall be able to go to other worlds some day, then aliens may well be coming here right now.

Earthly saucers
Some people think that the small number of UFO's that cannot be accounted for in any other way are indeed nuts-and-bolts craft — but not from space. When structured craft are sighted, they claim that these are experimental military prototypes, or misidentifications of ordinary aircraft. This argument has been used since the beginning of the flying saucer era.

Before 1947 there was a wave of reports of "ghost rockets" in Scandinavia. Research put these down to the Soviet Union testing captured Nazi V-weapons. This was an explanation used in the late 1940's to account for some of the craft seen in the American West, where German scientists had been relocated to work on the U.S.A.'s space program.

A French flying saucer
This airship was built by Jean Grimaldi of Normandy, France, in 1962. It had two engines driving two vertical and two horizontal propellers, and the inventor claimed that it could fly at 100 m.p.h.

W. Harbinson's novel *Genesis* produces some evidence that Nazis scientists were working on the development of circular aircraft toward the end of the Second World War. In a factual afterword, the author notes from his research that a saucer-shaped device supposedly built at the BMW plant in Prague in 1944 actually test-flew in February 1945. Apparently it was destroyed, despite its apparent success, in order to prevent it from falling into the hands of the Allies.

According to Harbinson, this craft was driven by advanced jet propulsion. It was nearly 140 feet in diameter and shaped like a discus with a fixed cupola covering a cockpit in the center. It had adjustable wings that rotated around the dome. Harbinson quotes reliable air force sources from Britain and the U.S.A. on what was found when the secret bases in Germany were first captured in 1945. These are

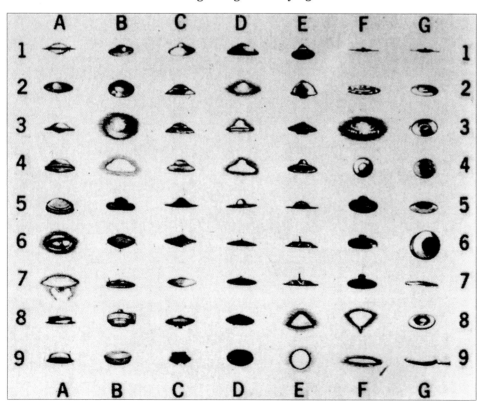

CRASHED SAUCERS

Is there really any truth in the rumors of alien spacecraft crash-landing in the U.S.A.?

A FIERCE STORM raged across the desert near Roswell, New Mexico, on the night of July 2, 1947. The following morning W.W. "Mac" Brazel found strange debris scattered over a large area of his ranch. This consisted of a tinfoil-like substance, strands of wire, small metallic rods covered with undecipherable writing, and pieces of parchment-like paper. Brazel collected a few scraps and gave them to the local sheriff, who contacted Roswell Army Air Field.

This was then the home of the world's only atomic attack unit, the 509th Bomb Group. Col. William Blanchard, commander of the 509th, responded with alacrity. He ordered Maj. Jesse A. Marcel, the group's intelligence officer, and a civilian member of the Counter Intelligence Corps (CIC) to investigate.

They spent a day at Brazel's ranch, collecting the debris and loading it into a station wagon and a jeep to take it back to the base. In 1978, shortly before his death, Marcel told researchers into this incident that the debris was "nothing made on earth." According to Marcel, the tinfoil-like substance could neither be burnt with a blowtorch nor dented with a 16-pound sledgehammer.

Four small bodies

At about the same time, and over 100 miles away, Grady L. Barnett came upon what he thought was a crashed flying disc. Beside it lay four small dead bodies. They had frail limbs, and disproportionately large heads with big, slanted eyes. According to Barnett, their bodies were encased in tight, one-piece, gray suits with no visible fastenings.

Here too, the military was quickly on the scene. Barnett and another group of witnesses were ushered away and ordered not to speak about the incident. Shortly afterward, on July 8, 1947, an official press release, approved by a Lt. Walter Haut, announced that the flying saucer mystery had been solved, and that saucer debris had been recovered by the 509th Bomb Group. Within hours, however, that press release had been canceled. The debris from both incidents was reportedly loaded onto a B-29 and flown to Carswell Air Force Base in Fort Worth, Texas, where Brig. Gen. Roger Ramey, commander of the Eighth Air Force, called a press conference. The flying saucer, Ramey explained, was nothing more exotic than the remains of a standard weather balloon.

A government cover-up?

Roswell is merely the best-documented of a number of accounts of crashed saucers, hastily retrieved by the U.S. Air Force. In many cases autopsies are said to have been performed on the bodies of the deceased alien occupants. Speculation about the extent of the cover-up forced the military to institute some form of inquiry into the UFO phenomenon, and in January 1948 the U.S. Air Force set up Project Sign.

Crash victim?
In 1951 a newspaper in Cologne, Germany, published this photograph. It purported to show the victim of a flying saucer crash-landing near Mexico City. The figure is around 28 inches tall, and is wearing a loincloth. The newspaper later admitted that the photograph was an April Fool's Day hoax. The "alien" was probably a wax model, or possibly the shaved body of a monkey.

Saucer debris
U.S. Air Corps officers inspect the remains of the mysterious object that crashed in a storm at Roswell, New Mexico, in 1947. The material was subjected to various tests, and one of the investigating officers was convinced that the object was of unearthly origin.

Experimental flying car
This strange-looking craft was built by Paul Moller, and is the culmination of a 20-year project. The Moller 200X had its first untethered test-flight in 1986, and reached a height of 35 feet.

consistent in their reports of the construction of prototypes of unusual high-performance craft.

An acute lack of stability
The aero-engineering company A.V. Roe also used jet propulsion in a project named Avrocar that it developed during the 1950's for the U.S. Air Force. Prototypes of a flying-saucer-shaped

There are also practical problems for any passengers in such a craft. Many UFO's appear to defy the laws of inertia, for example, making right-angle turns or slowing from great speeds to a standstill. The laws of physics suggest that human bodies could not survive the forces generated by such maneuvers.

If alien spacecraft do exist, it may be that they are powered in totally different ways from our own. We even have some clues about the nature of these power sources. Many reports tell of motor vehicles impeded by close proximity to a UFO. This effect often dims or extinguishes lighting and stalls engines. This suggests a force field generated by the UFO that impedes the ionic flow within electrical circuits. It appears not to be simple electromagnetic radiation, because this would leave a magnetic

---

It may be that alien spacecraft are powered in a totally different way from our own.

---

signature on the metal body of the car. This has not been found when tested for.

The "falling leaf" effect gives another hint as to how flying saucers may be powered. UFO's are often described as descending in a curious manner, like a leaf falling from a tree. You can simulate this by dropping a saucer into a tank of water; it will slide from side to side as it sinks to the bottom.

A study of the physics of such movement suggests that, like the saucer in the water, the UFO becomes virtually massless during its descent. If alien technology can make matter massless, the problem of the destructive inertial effects of high maneuverability is solved too. Massless passengers would not suffer from inertia.

A number of engineers have tried to use this sort of information to design a UFO on paper. An American chemist

UFO maneuverability
This visualization from the popular 1950's magazine Weird Science-Fantasy *shows one example of UFO's performing an astonishing feat (in this case a sharp right-angle turn) well beyond the capability of our own flying machines.*

aircraft were built, but apparently they demonstrated an acute lack of stability.

These trials did show that there were major difficulties understanding how the flying-saucer shape flew within our atmosphere. Saucers, if they truly exist, appear not to use the same kind of technology as either our jet-propelled airplanes or our rockets.

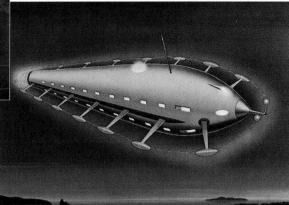

Different types of craft?
These illustrations of alien spacecraft sightings show how diverse are the designs reported.

NUTS-AND-BOLTS SAUCERS
If some UFO's are indeed alien spacecraft they do not conform to any one particular design. Comparing the various types of supersonic jet aircraft, or the NASA space shuttle with its Soviet counterpart, it is obvious that the form of the end product is fairly limited by human engineering constraints.

All shapes and sizes
UFO's, by contrast, come in all shapes and sizes. Among those that look like machines, the archetypal saucer with a dome on top is most common, but there are many other types. There are reports of cigars, cones, spindles, eggs, manta rays, and almost any other form imaginable.

Another difficulty to remember when assessing UFO's as spacecraft is that we see them within our atmosphere, not outer space. If they are indeed extraterrestrial machines then they have presumably been designed to fly through the air, as well as through outer space. However, many of the shapes described do not share aerodynamic design principles with our own spacecraft.

The evidence against
Coming up with a plausible design that can fly equally well in space and in the earth's atmosphere continues to challenge scientists, and no one can satisfactorily explain flying saucers' extreme maneuverability. There are no convincing photographs of alien spaceships at close quarters. Despite a number of reported saucer crashes, there is not a single piece of material evidence that shows indications of being of extraterrestrial origin.

and engineering consultant, Kenneth Behrendt, has devised the anti-mass field (AMF) theory to construct a complex mathematical blueprint of a craft that would prevent mass field radiation, effectively rendering the machine gravity-free. This is a much more sophisticated approach to the sometimes impractical "anti-gravity" ideas which have been proposed for many years and which are of wildly varying levels of practicality.

Gyroscopic propulsion systems
One of the interesting points of Behrendt's theory is that such a craft would ionize the surrounding atmosphere. This would provoke effects that are identical to those that are frequently reported by UFO witnesses. The circular design of Behrendt's craft also fits in with reports of sightings.

Prof. Eric Laithwaite of Imperial College in London has made no secret of his interest in the UFO field as a possible source of ideas for research. He worked on the linear induction motor, which uses magnetic field principles, and which is being successfully built into hover-train projects throughout the world. Laithwaite has some very advanced ideas on how to reduce mass and attain immense speeds by using gyroscopic propulsion systems. He plans to test them fully in space through experiments aboard the space shuttle.

The USAF Avrocar

INSIDE
THE SPACECRAFT

What do alien spacecraft look like inside? The testimony of those who claim to have been abducted by aliens suggests that they vary as much as the interiors of our homes. But certain features seem to recur with uncanny consistency.

FRANCK FONTAINE claimed to have been abducted by alien beings in Cergy-Pontoise, France, in November 1979. He found it difficult to recall the experience and was reluctant to discuss it in detail. However, he did talk about lying on a kind of couch in a large white room with machines around the walls. All the machines were the same height and had white glass fronts that lit up from time to time.

This tallies with the description given by Ted, one of the alleged abductees hypnotically regressed by Dr. Edith Fiore. His story is in her book, *Abductions* (1989).

"I'm in a room in some kind of craft. And the room is round and there's lights and dials along the wall. On one side there's all kinds of dials and lights in little screens....The room is small....I have a feeling like it's maybe about 12 feet across. Maybe from the floor to the ceiling it's also about 12 feet. It's very clean, very smooth, and it's domed. There's almost no furniture in it except for the panels of lights and this table that contours around the room."

The machinery and the lights are a recurring theme in abductee accounts. The rooms inside the spaceships are sometimes round or oval, and often have domed ceilings. In another of Dr. Fiore's case histories, Sandi was taken aboard a spacecraft by aliens, and she later described her surroundings.

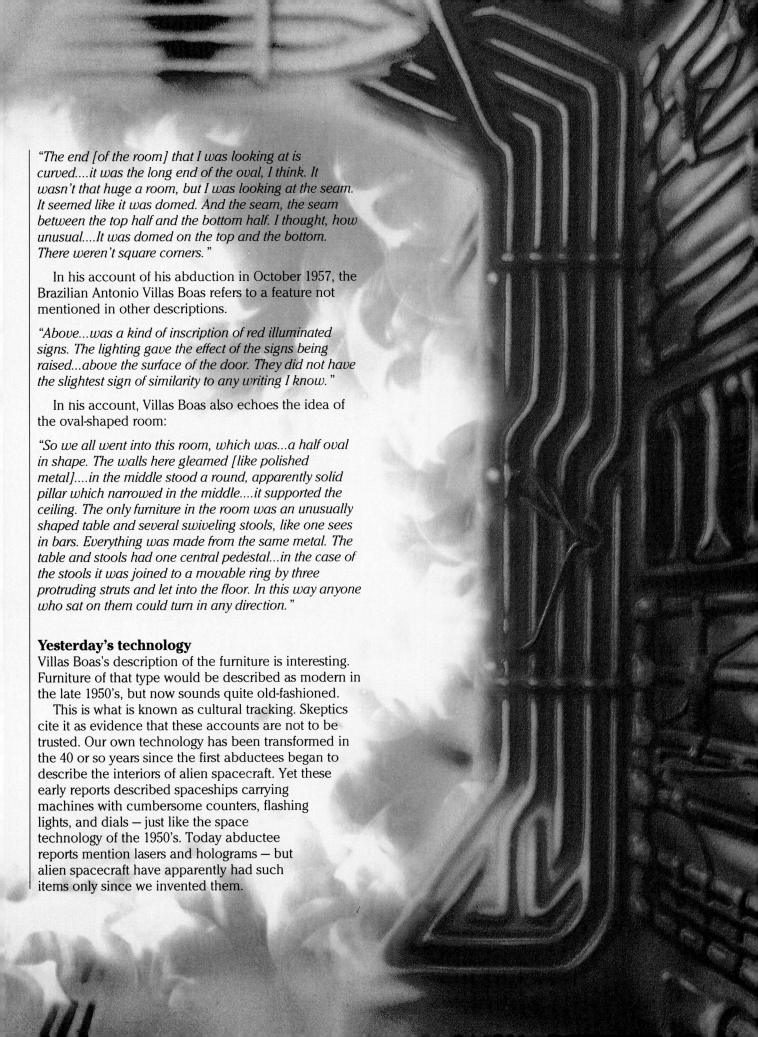

"The end [of the room] that I was looking at is curved....it was the long end of the oval, I think. It wasn't that huge a room, but I was looking at the seam. It seemed like it was domed. And the seam, the seam between the top half and the bottom half. I thought, how unusual....It was domed on the top and the bottom. There weren't square corners."

In his account of his abduction in October 1957, the Brazilian Antonio Villas Boas refers to a feature not mentioned in other descriptions.

"Above...was a kind of inscription of red illuminated signs. The lighting gave the effect of the signs being raised...above the surface of the door. They did not have the slightest sign of similarity to any writing I know."

In his account, Villas Boas also echoes the idea of the oval-shaped room:

"So we all went into this room, which was...a half oval in shape. The walls here gleamed [like polished metal]....in the middle stood a round, apparently solid pillar which narrowed in the middle....it supported the ceiling. The only furniture in the room was an unusually shaped table and several swiveling stools, like one sees in bars. Everything was made from the same metal. The table and stools had one central pedestal...in the case of the stools it was joined to a movable ring by three protruding struts and let into the floor. In this way anyone who sat on them could turn in any direction."

Yesterday's technology

Villas Boas's description of the furniture is interesting. Furniture of that type would be described as modern in the late 1950's, but now sounds quite old-fashioned.

This is what is known as cultural tracking. Skeptics cite it as evidence that these accounts are not to be trusted. Our own technology has been transformed in the 40 or so years since the first abductees began to describe the interiors of alien spacecraft. Yet these early reports described spaceships carrying machines with cumbersome counters, flashing lights, and dials — just like the space technology of the 1950's. Today abductee reports mention lasers and holograms — but alien spacecraft have apparently had such items only since we invented them.

CHAPTER THREE

CONTACT WITH THE VISITORS

Soon after the first sightings of flying saucers came reports of encounters with beings aboard them — described as wise and gentle. But, in time, the friendly visitors seemed to be replaced by a more sinister breed....

The universe may contain other worlds than ours; those worlds may be inhabited; the inhabitants of those worlds may be making efforts to contact us. Humankind has toyed with these ideas for centuries. But only since the early 1950's has it been seriously suggested that such contact has indeed taken place.

Reports of mysterious lights in the sky are not, of course, anything new. But flying saucers are a modern phenomenon, and claims of contact with alien visitors were rare until our own times. Once a belief in flying saucers as extraterrestrial spacecraft

"Little Boy"
Atom bomb of the type dropped on Hiroshima in August 1945.

BAN-THE-BOMB ALIENS

James Lipp, a member of the Project Sign team set up by the U.S. Army Air Force to investigate UFO's, wrote in a report of December 1948: "The Martians have kept a long-term watch on Earth and have been alarmed by the sight of our A-bomb shots as evidence that we are warlike and on the threshold of space travel."

It is clear from the context that the writer intended this simply as speculation. He did, however, go to the trouble of checking whether or not the five atom bombs that had been exploded by that date would have been visible from Mars. (The answers to that question are two yes, two no, and one possibly.)

Spying saucers

Many UFO's were reported appearing in the neighborhood of U.S. Army Air Force bases where atomic weapons were stored. This fact seemed to suggest to UFO enthusiasts that the aliens were indeed interested in the U.S.A.'s nuclear program. Another, more mundane, explanation is that the UFO's may have been top-secret experimental aircraft from these bases on test flights, which the U.S. Army Air Force was not prepared to acknowledge.

became widespread, it was only a matter of time before reports came in of their occupants being sighted, and in due course people actually claimed to have met the aliens.

A visitor from Venus

In September 1953 British author Desmond Leslie published *Flying Saucers Have Landed,* a chronicle of flying saucer sightings. The final section of the book, contributed by Leslie's American coauthor, George Adamski, was quite sensational. If Adamski was telling the truth, a new era had dawned: humankind had at last made contact with people from other worlds.

Adamski claimed that he had met a visitor from Venus. In this and subsequent writings, he explained that he had been chosen by the aliens to be their contact on earth. It was not long before others were telling how they, too, had been selected. Within a few years there were a number of "contactees," as they were called, each with a different story of their meetings with the aliens.

What was surprising was that no two contactees encountered the same aliens. It seemed that several space peoples had

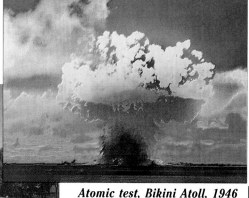

Atomic test, Bikini Atoll, 1946
This false-color photograph shows the massive release of energy in a nuclear explosion. Under the right conditions, it would be visible from another planet in the solar system.

Atomic test, Nevada, 1952

decided, at more or less the same moment, to make themselves known to humankind. Each group of aliens had chosen to contact a different person — generally an American, usually male, nearly always white.

The visitors themselves provided the reason for choosing this moment in human history. They were alarmed by humankind's discovery of nuclear energy. Now that it possessed the capability to destroy the world, the human race had become a menace to the entire universe.

There were features of the contactees' stories that made them less than convincing, and they were soon in decline. After a period in demand as fun guests on talk shows, many faded from the scene. A few managed to retain enough credibility to acquire a following of loyal devotees.

The human race had become a menace to the entire universe.

In the 1960's a new phenomenon began to be reported, and this has continued up to the present day. It appeared to signal a change of tactics on the part of the visitors. Instead of contacting chosen individuals with the intention of forging cultural links with humankind, the aliens were now less friendly, more forceful, and displayed an alarming interest in human biology.

Tours of the solar system

In a typical contactee case, the individual claimed to have been invited aboard a spacecraft, where he or she was treated politely, offered delightful drinks, and given instructive tours of the solar system. Today's witnesses, the "abductees," are reportedly being taken against their will onto alien spacecraft in what amounts to kidnap. The aliens generally subject them to a rigorous physical examination. The experience is said to be unpleasant, and even traumatic — especially so when, as is sometimes claimed, the process goes beyond examination, and aliens take blood and tissue samples. They have even been accused of placing mysterious implants in the abductees' bodies. They are also said to be pursuing genetic experiments, and in some cases, to have had sexual intercourse with humans. Some female abductees claim that they have borne several hybrid children, but the babies have been taken from them to be raised on the aliens' own planet.

Human genetic potential

Such extraterrestrial coupling did not start with the abductees: as far back as 1954, according to South African contactee Elizabeth Klarer, she had sexual relations with an alien, and produced a son as a result. In her case, the experience was entirely pleasant — indeed, ecstatically so. It is interesting that her upbeat story was not widely believed, whereas many people have been prepared more recently to credit the abductees' alarming stories.

From these stories arose a theory that aliens were no longer concerned with human culture or creativity, and had transferred their attentions to the genetic potential of the human race as a biological species. One alarming inference to be drawn from this is that they are planning some global onslaught on humanity, either to enslave us or to replace us with hybrid beings acclimatized to earthly conditions. Once again, there are many alternative theories, all more or less horrific.

Those investigators who believe that the abduction stories are literally true insist that they have nothing in common with the contactee stories — the latter were mere fantasy, they say, while the abductions are real. This is hard to believe, given the fact that both are occurring in the same historical era, both are related to UFO's, and both have many other features in common.

In neither case do we have any concrete evidence that the event actually occurred. The abductees are definitely experiencing something, but then that was also true of many of the contactees. The question is whether the claims of the abductees should be taken at face value. If not, the investigation must center on the psychological experience, and why it is becoming so common. The question of the reality of abduction by aliens has divided investigators more than any other single issue in the history of UFO research.

Fact or fiction?
The cover of A Trip to Mars *by Fenton Ash, published in 1909, presented Martians as benevolent, angelic figures. This perception was echoed by the contactee reports of the 1950's, which purported to answer the questions everyone was asking. The crucial mystery was taken by Gordon Cove as the title of his book on the subject:* Who Pilots the Flying Saucers? *Soon afterwards, the aliens lost their friendly attributes and became, for many, a force to be feared.*

CLASSIFYING CLOSE ENCOUNTERS

In his book *The UFO Experience: A Scientific Inquiry*, Dr. J. Allen Hynek introduced a simple system of classifying UFO reports that has come into universal usage. He defines a UFO close encounter as one where the object comes within an estimated 500 feet of the witness. These close encounters are subdivided into three categories:

The First Kind

This is the simplest encounter. The UFO is seen at close range (within 500 feet), but does not affect the environment. Witnesses commonly report seeing a disc that hovers above the ground and then accelerates rapidly away.

The Second Kind

These encounters have definite physical effects upon both animate and inanimate objects. Typically, the rotating

spacecraft ascends vertically from the ground and leaves vegetation flattened and scorched. Animals in the vicinity become alarmed. Witnesses report that car engines stall, radios stop playing, and headlights are dimmed.

The Third Kind

In these cases individuals actually see the occupants of the craft. Virtually all happen at night, and there are usually only one or two witnesses. Generally the aliens do not try to communicate, but retreat into their craft.

Dr. Hynek thought that this category should not include contactee cases. He defined these as reports of a "favored" human intermediary frequently sighting UFO's, and always having a communication from the aliens to relay to the human race.

Close Encounters of the Third Kind — *the movie*

THE CONTACTEES

The arrival of the "space brothers" proved that the occupants of the UFO's were friendly. This was the message spread by those who believed themselves chosen as the aliens' contacts on earth.

Daniel Fry
Fry said he was first contacted in July 1950 in New Mexico, then flown in a spacecraft to New York and back in half an hour.

BRIEF ENCOUNTER

The blond, long-haired Venusian whom Adamski claimed to have met in the California desert in 1952 was called Orthon. Adamski described him as follows:

"He was round faced with an extremely high forehead; large, but calm, grey-green eyes, slightly aslant at the outer corners; with slightly higher cheek bones than an Occidental, but not so high as an Indian or an Oriental; a finely chiseled nose, not conspicuously large; and an average size mouth with beautiful white teeth that shone when he smiled or spoke."

An awesome presence

Adamski's reaction was similar to that of most contactees:

"I felt like a child in the presence of one with great wisdom and much love, and I became very humble within myself...for from him was radiating a feeling of infinite understanding and kindness, with supreme humility."

AS THE NUMBERS OF UFO sightings continued to increase in the 1950's, the theory that they were extraterrestrial spacecraft soon came to dominate all discussion of the topic. Throughout that decade an increasing number of people claimed to have had contact with the occupants of UFO's. These extraterrestrial visitors readily offered answers to the questions that everyone was asking: Why are the flying saucers visiting our planet? Who is piloting them? Where have they come from?

The first contactees emerged from the strange network of religious and occultist groups that even in the 1940's characterized the social landscape of Southern California. This area was not far from U.S. military test sites and defense installations in the desert areas of Arizona, New Mexico, and Nevada — sites of the first atom bomb tests. Several early UFO incidents were reported from this region, supporting the popular theory that the extraterrestrials were taking an interest in earth's military capacity.

Great physical beauty

Contactees such as George Adamski, Daniel Fry, and Truman Bethurum told variations of the same story. They reported seeing saucers on the ground and meeting their crews in sparsely populated desert regions. The "space people" they met were very like humans, and were usually distinguished by their air of authority or their great physical beauty. Many contactees described tall, blond Nordic types dressed in one-piece ski suits. Most of the men had shoulder-length hair, which was unheard-of in the 1950's.

According to the contactees, the alien visitors were eager to communicate. They had indeed been monitoring nuclear tests and humankind's first attempts at space travel, and had now come to warn us that we were upsetting the balance of the universe. In some cases the aliens took the role of missionaries, bringing new philosophical and religious ideas to humanity. Their apparent benevolence led some of the first contactees to call them the "space brothers."

Friendliness was the feature that distinguished the contactees from other witnesses of the activities of UFO

George Adamski
Adamski named his first contact as Orthon, a Venusian, whom he met in November 1952 in California. Adamski claimed also to have visited Mars and Saturn.

Orthon the Venusian
One of the witnesses of Adamski's encounter, Alice Wells, made a sketch of the friendly visitor, on which this color painting is based.

Howard and Marla Menger
Howard claimed originally to be from Saturn. He met and married 500-year-old Marla from Venus in 1958. He later withdrew his story.

WE MET THE SPACE PEOPLE

THE STORY OF THE MITCHELL SISTERS
BY HELEN and BETTY MITCHELL

$1.00

SAUCERIAN PUBLICATIONS, CLARKSBURG, W.VA.

Helen and Betty Mitchell
The Mitchell sisters said they met two men from Mars in 1957, in Missouri; and that later they met a Venusian, and Helen went for a ride in a spacecraft.

Claude Vorilhon ("Rael")
The Frenchman Vorilhon took the name Rael after his UFO experiences. In one encounter he reported taking a bath with five female robots.

Truman Bethurum
Bethurum said he met an alien woman named Aura Rhanes in July 1952 in California. She was a spacecraft captain from the planet Clarion.

George King
London taxi-driver King was first contacted by a disembodied voice in May 1954. He later said he met a Martian named Mars Sector Six, and a Venusian called Jesus Christ.

Buck Nelson
Nelson claimed he saw UFO's in July 1954 over his home in Missouri, and that in April 1955 he rode on a spaceship to the Moon, Mars, and Venus.

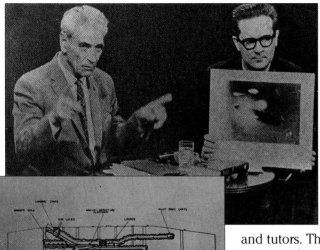

VENUSIAN SPACECRAFT
(MOTHER-SHIP)

Talk-show contactee
Adamski is interviewed by radio personality Long John Nebel, who is holding one of his UFO photographs. Adamski claimed to have learned enough about this Venusian interplanetary carrier to commission a technical drawing of it (inset). Nebel interviewed many UFO contactees, and his verdict on their tales was: "I don't buy any of these bits."

Desmond Leslie
Adamski's coauthor of the book Flying Saucers Have Landed, *Leslie delved into the past to show that alien spacecraft had been reported from time to time since the beginning of recorded history.*

occupants. Later reports would tell of encounters with creatures who shunned contact, were indifferent, or even hostile to humans. But the space brothers were thought to be our guides and tutors. They gave clear answers about why they were here. They also said where they had come from. In most cases, they had apparently traveled from Earth's neighboring planets — Mars or Venus — and seldom from anywhere outside our solar system. Some claimed that they came from the planet Clarion. This, they said, was a member of our solar system that had not been discovered because it orbited on the opposite side of the sun from the earth.

After the initial encounter, which was usually accidental, subsequent meetings might be arranged by the space people themselves, often by telepathic communication. It was not unusual for someone to claim several dozen encounters. Often he or she would claim to have been invited on board the UFO to be shown details of its construction, or even taken on a trip to the visitors' home planet.

Quasi-religious cults

Although the contactee phenomenon started in America, and had its greatest influence in California, it spread globally. Many contactees wrote books about their encounters. Several set up quasi-religious cults based on the philosophical messages of their guides. Most of these folded with the death or decline into obscurity of their founders. One that was still going in the 1990's was the Aetherius Society, with branches in the U.S.A. and Britain. This was set up by George King, a former London taxi-driver who claimed to have received telepathic messages from space people (including one from a Venusian named Jesus Christ). Most of the surviving groups are now involved in esoteric philosophy or "channeling."

Space exploration

The stories of the contactees became increasingly untenable with the advance of space research and exploration. The stories of humanlike creatures living on nearby planets could be demonstrated to be untrue by improved telescopes and then by the first space probes. By 1969 it was impossible for anyone to come forward with a story claiming a visit to an inhabited and fertile Moon or Mars. Indeed, the era of the contactees is neatly bounded by the raising of interest in interplanetary flight in the 1940's, and the achievement of this goal in the 1960's. The first gave birth to the contactees' hopes; the latter dealt a death blow to their dreams.

Similarly, the philosophical messages and cosmic warnings were eventually exposed as a string of platitudes. In some cases, the space brothers had confided high-tech information to the contactees. However, public demonstrations of such scientific advances as UFO power sources, miracle cures, even self-heating boots in one case, never seemed to work when organized by enthusiastic earthlings.

A closed book

The contactee phenomenon is seen by most UFO researchers today as a closed book, and something quite apart from the general trends of serious UFO investigation. There is little in it that connects with the abduction reports that are the basis of most modern UFO researchers' investigations. Few of the contactees ever offered any other evidence than their own individual testimony, sometimes backed up by other members of their cults.

The contactee story is part of a long mythical tradition of meetings between humans and benevolent creatures from other places, who profess to be able to

The contactees wanted to spread news of their encounters.

help us and guide our destiny. It perhaps has more to do with the types of contacts and messages that are reported by spiritualist mediums than it does with the wider range of UFO occupant reports featuring non-human entities.

Simplistic solutions

Most of the contactees had something in common: before their encounter they were powerless, perhaps slightly alienated people, who had the feeling that they were being swept along by forces beyond their control. In the 1950's, at the height of the cold war, with the U.S.A. and the Soviet Union engaged in a frightening arms race, the simplistic solutions of the space brothers looked appealing. Benevolent extraterrestrials entrusted the contactee with the secrets of the universe, sometimes even appointing him or her the space people's envoy on earth. This put the contactee into a position of imaginary power – sometimes with a degree of real power over other cult followers – and helped fill a spiritual or emotional gap in his or her life.

Although there were some hoaxes, most of the contactees were perfectly genuine in reporting events that they sincerely believed had happened. But in retrospect there is little doubt that these events were of an internal, psychological nature. As none of the contacts was seen by anyone except the contactee's followers, we have no objective account of events.

The greatest mystery of the contactees is the nature of the mental process that produced their reports. Was it simply delusion, self-deception, and misinterpretation? Or is there some other mechanism that can produce images of fantastic and utopian worlds in human minds? If so, it has implications far beyond the historical curiosity of the contactees themselves.

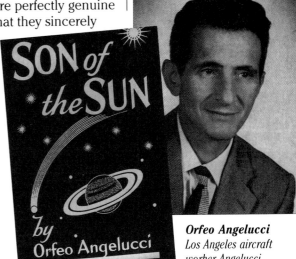

Orfeo Angelucci
Los Angeles aircraft worker Angelucci claimed that he was contacted by "a man and woman near a possible ultimate of perfection." They communicated telepathically their anxiety about "the creeping menace of Communism." Angelucci published an account of his experiences, titled Son of the Sun.

SCI-FI CONNECTION

How much science fiction influences reports of UFO's and their occupants has not been resolved. For example, the story of the abduction of Betty and Barney Hill was made into a TV film called *The UFO Incident* and transmitted in October 1975. Shortly afterward there was a notable upsurge in the number of abductions reported. On the other hand, the movie *Close Encounters of the Third Kind* was released in the U.S.A. in late 1977, and had no obvious effect on the numbers of alleged extraterrestrial events.

Where are the robots?

Some elements from science fiction tend to appear in UFO reports, while others do not. For example, as in a film studio, lighting in alien spacecraft is often said to have no obvious source, and to cast no shadows; as in all TV sci-fi, spacecraft doors described in abduction reports operate automatically. On the other hand, it might be expected that features of perhaps the best-known sci-fi alien, Mr. Spock from *Star Trek*, would be reflected in some accounts, but he is not obviously recognizable in any of the many descriptions of UFO occupants. Robots, a great favorite of sci-fi, seldom appear either, nor do, as a general rule, the grisly panoply of monsters that sci-fi writers have managed to invent over the years.

The aliens' motives seem to owe little to sci-fi. They never say that they want to take over our world

and force humankind into slavery, although this has been a basic plot since the beginning of the sci-fi genre. Their actions could, however, be taken to indicate an interest in genetic experiments with humans, the theory being that this is their strategy to dominate our world; but it is a far less common subject in fiction.

Sci-fi magazine cover, 1950
The contactees saw the extraterrestrial visitors as wise and gentle humanoids with the interests of our planet at heart. This is in contrast to the view of most sci-fi, in which aliens are usually a threat to humankind.

Sci-fi magazine cover, 1967

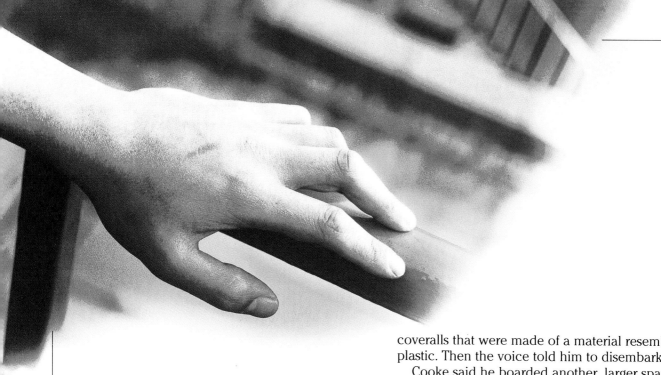

CASEBOOK
JAMES COOKE

A railed ramp descended from the craft, and a disembodied voice told him to jump.

ON SEPTEMBER 6, 1957, James Cooke of Runcorn, England, received what he called a telepathic message saying he should visit a nearby hill that night to meet space people. He had claimed many previous UFO sightings, but nothing, he said, had prepared him for what was to follow.

He claimed that at 2:15 A.M., on a hill overlooking the town, he saw a blindingly illuminated spacecraft hovering a few inches above the ground 20 yards in front of him. He watched the craft change colors from blue to white, then to blue again before it finally turned a dark red.

A light that cast no shadows

The spacecraft came to rest a couple of feet from Cooke. A railed ramp descended from the craft, and a disembodied voice told him to jump — not step up — onto the ramp, as the ground was wet from rain. "Don't keep a foot on the ground or you will be hurt," instructed the voice. Cooke said he did as he was told, and found himself inside the craft. A dazzling light that cast no shadows illuminated everything. The voice told him to undress and put on some one-piece seamless

coveralls that were made of a material resembling plastic. Then the voice told him to disembark.

Cooke said he boarded another, larger spacecraft that had landed nearby, and there encountered about 20 alien humanoids, who communicated with him telepathically. He was taken to the aliens' home planet, Zomdic, in another solar system. "Your scientists don't know this planet exists," he was told.

Zomdic appeared to Cooke to be an ideal society: "They do not use money. What they need they have. Energy is turned into matter in any required form."

Like other contactees, James Cooke received a message from one of the "Wise Men" of the planet Zomdic: "The inhabitants of your planet will upset the balance if they persist in using force instead of harmony. Warn them of the danger."

"But they won't listen to me," protested Cooke.

"Or to anyone else either," replied the Wise Man.

After this meeting the aliens returned him to the ship for his journey home. When leaving the craft, he forgot the aliens' earlier admonition and stepped onto the ground before removing his hand from the rail of the ramp. Later he found his hand had been burned.

Healing powers

He related his story to the British UFO Association, and when Thelma Roberts from *Flying Saucer Review* interviewed him for an article in the May 1958 issue of the magazine, he showed her a burn on his hand. Cooke continued to receive telepathic messages from his space visitors for some time, he said.

Cooke also claimed to have gained healing powers from his contact with the aliens. In June 1961 he founded a sect in Runcorn called the Church of Aquarius, whose mission was to bring about universal peace. It drew enough followers to require the opening of a second church in the town. James Cooke himself disappeared one December afternoon in 1969, since when he has never been seen again. The cult did not survive long after his disappearance.

GEORGE ADAMSKI

The only trace of an alien that remained was a footprint marked with indecipherable symbols.

ON NOVEMBER 20, 1952, George Adamski walked into the desert near Desert Center, California. He returned some hours later to tell of his astounding meeting with a handsome long-haired alien. Adamski said that, communicating by sign language and telepathy, he learned that the visitor was called Orthon, and was from the planet Venus. His mission was to warn humankind that radiation from atomic testing was endangering the universe. Adamski's experience remains the first fully documented contactee encounter of the flying saucer era.

Date with destiny
Adamski had made several visits to desert areas where flying saucers were reported to have landed. On this occasion he was accompanied by six companions. As they stopped by the roadside to eat, they thought they saw a spaceship land. Adamski became excited. He said that this ship had come for him, and he must not keep it waiting. One of his companions drove him close to where the craft appeared to have landed, and he walked into the desert toward it. From where they watched, his friends claimed they saw an alien being. One woman observed the being through a telescope and made an on-the-spot drawing. After an hour, Adamski returned to his friends. The only trace of an alien that remained after the incident was a footprint marked with indecipherable symbols, of which they took a plaster cast. All six witnesses later signed an affidavit that attested to the truth of what they had seen.

Polish-born Adamski's interest in mysticism and otherworldly things began well before his first alien encounter. In the 1930's he had founded a mystical cult called the Royal Order of Tibet, at Laguna Beach, California. At the time of his first meeting with Orthon, he had found work (as a hamburger chef) near the giant Mount Palomar telescope in California.

Interplanetary ambassador
In 1953 Adamski wrote of his experience in *Flying Saucers Have Landed*, coauthored with Desmond Leslie, followed two years later by *Inside the Spaceships*. The latter book told the even more remarkable tale of his voyages in a Venusian flying saucer to other planets in the solar system. Adamski reported that most of the planets he visited, and also the moon, were inhabited.

The aliens he encountered would not let themselves be photographed. Adamski did, however, produce photographs of the Venusians' "scout ships." However, these proved to be fakes: the craft were models made from chicken feeders and bottle coolers.

Adamski also described his attendance at an interplanetary council of the advanced civilizations of the solar system, to which the planet earth would be admitted when its inhabitants had reached a suitable spiritual level. Adamski believed that he was the council's ambassador on earth.

A charismatic man
Adamski was a charismatic man who soon established a large following. He traveled the world on lecture tours, meeting with dignitaries and heads of state, including Queen Juliana of the Netherlands and, his followers claimed, Pope John XXIII. He died in 1965 before the space program conclusively disproved his assertion that there was life on other planets in our solar system. By then his cult, called the George Adamski Foundation, was well established. It still flourishes today in California and has a membership of several thousands worldwide.

ABDUCTION!

Imagine that you are driving along a country road late at night, tired and in a hurry to get home. Ahead of you, you notice a bright light in the sky — a star or a plane, perhaps. It comes closer and closer, and you suddenly realize that it is a strange disc-shaped craft, glowing weirdly....

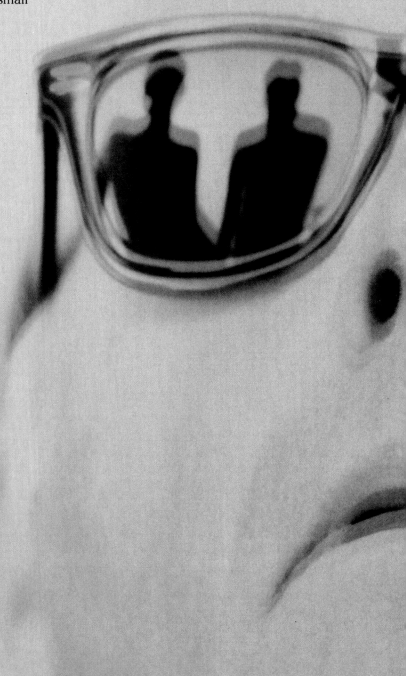

THE NEXT THING YOU REMEMBER, you are sitting in your car, staring at the shapes of three figures looking in at you. But these could not possibly be human beings. Their heads are huge, their bodies small and thin. There is something quite terrifying about their eyes: huge black wells that seem ready to swallow you up. Without knowing how you got there, you are now inside the strange craft, in a room that appears to be lit from everywhere and nowhere. You are lying on a couch, unable to move, and the creatures are standing around you. They move instruments over you. You feel a stabbing pain as something is pushed hard into your nose. You recall no more until you find yourself back in your car, trying to make some sense of what has just happened. Instinctively you are not trying too hard. At the back of your mind is the disturbing feeling that you have met these creatures and their machines before, and that you will meet them again.

Psychological tests

This experience, or close variations of it, has been reported by thousands of people. They are not insane. Many have undergone psychological tests. The results show little deviation, if any, from standard mental profiles. There is little doubt that the people who give these accounts are sincere. Their stories are internally consistent and bear each other out to a remarkable degree. These people are the abductees. There are many of them, and their number is growing.

It is hard to pinpoint exactly when the abduction phenomenon began. Stories of contacts with UFO crews arose in the early 1950's. Most of the contactees welcomed the encounter. They hoped to learn from the aliens and often felt that they had been "chosen" as a particular honor. But gradually the era of the contactees came to an end. Increasingly people who reported seeing the

occupants of UFO's told of inhuman, grotesque creatures: small-bodied, large-headed, uncommunicative, even hostile. From space brothers who were helping us, they became aliens who were observing us.

Many abduction cases, particularly early in the 1960's, still included some features of the friendlier contactee cases. Sometimes the abductee was lectured on the problems facing humankind, and warned of the apocalyptic end toward which we were steering our planet.

A positive experience

Unlike the frightening and hostile experience of many recent abductions, some of the earlier abductees were influenced positively by the messages they received. Some found that on their return to "normality" they tried to act on the advice and revelations they received, and altered their lifestyle — sometimes radically for the better. An Argentine builder, Gilbert Ciccioli, had a typical experience in 1974, which began, he claimed, when a blinding white light woke him up one night; he "returned" with an understanding of physics, astronomy, and philosophy — of which he had previously been ignorant.

Although there was no hard and fast line between abductees and contactees, researchers soon found one important difference. A very high proportion, perhaps half, of all the people who had experienced an abduction at first had no conscious recollection of it. They would

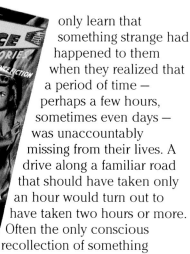
Sci-fi magazine cover, 1949

THE FACE OF THE ALIEN
The aliens' appearance as reported by abductees varies almost as widely as the representation of space monsters in science fiction. Skeptics have made much of the lack of uniformity in the aliens' appearance, suggesting that this is because they are based on images gleaned, consciously or subconsciously, from many sources, including science fiction.

"The Grays"
However, in America in the 1980's and early 1990's, abductees' descriptions of aliens began to sound more alike. Several types were described, but one began to predominate: the large-headed, big-eyed creatures known as "the Grays." But this may not reinforce the case for the physical reality of the aliens. It may be due to the subconscious assimilation by abductees of the proliferating images of this type of alien, which began to appear in the 1980's on book covers and film posters.

only learn that something strange had happened to them when they realized that a period of time — perhaps a few hours, sometimes even days — was unaccountably missing from their lives. A drive along a familiar road that should have taken only an hour would turn out to have taken two hours or more. Often the only conscious recollection of something unusual would be the memory of a lights-in-the-sky type of UFO sighting.

Fragmented memories
More details of the missing time might emerge through dreams or fragmented memories in the days and weeks following the event. However, UFO researchers soon discovered that hypnosis seemed to provide a shortcut to these hidden memories. Although about 40 percent of all abductees recall their experiences without hypnosis, hypnotic regression has since been used extensively, and has come to dominate the study of the abduction experience.

The use of hypnosis has proved problematic, however. The regression technique is useful for recovering lost memories, and has even been used in

> A period of time — perhaps a few hours, sometimes even days — was unaccountably missing from their lives.

forensic investigation, but it recovers not just forgotten events but also forgotten fantasies. Critics also fear that the regression process can be controlled by the hypnotist, who may consciously or accidentally ask leading questions to provoke a desired response. It is certainly not, as some researchers have claimed, a form of truth test.

Huge black eyes
Throughout the 1960's and 1970's abductees reported their experiences with a wide range of creatures. In different cases the captors were reported as looking, variously, totally human, robotic, or even like disembodied brains. One resembled the black monolith from the film *2001 — A Space Odyssey*. Others had mushroom-shaped heads. Often two different types of creatures would be reported working together.

However, by the end of the 1970's the cases were beginning to take on a more homogenous character. The majority of aliens involved were of the same type: small, gray-skinned, large-headed, with small mouths and no noses, and, most distinctively, huge black eyes that dominated their faces.

Throughout the 1980's a rift began to grow between ufologists on either side of the Atlantic, which reflected the different ways the phenomenon was developing in the U.S.A. and Europe. In America the abduction reports were dominated by the large-headed, big-eyed creatures — nicknamed "the Grays" — who, it appeared, were conducting human-alien hybridization experiments.

A real phenomenon?
Far fewer abduction cases seemed to have taken place among the larger European population, and those that were reported to have occurred involved a wider range of entities and activities than the American cases. European ufologists, with a few exceptions, tended to see the phenomenon in psychological and sociological terms, rather than as

"Flying Saucers" sci-fi comic, April 1967

HYPNOTIC REGRESSION

Dr. Martin T. Orne is a leading authority on hypnosis, and director of experimental psychiatry at the Institute of Pennsylvania Hospital. His extensive research on the use of hypnosis has led him to conclude that it is an unreliable tool for establishing what has actually happened in the past.

This has serious implications for the researchers who obtain stories of abductions from subjects under hypnosis. Many abductees have been regressed back to their childhood in an attempt to discover previous alien encounters. Orne comments that, under such hypnosis, "individuals will spontaneously elaborate a myriad of details which apparently could only be brought forth by someone actually observing the events as they transpired." This may cause the hypnotist to believe that the subject is really back in his or her childhood and recalling factual details.

Pseudo-memories

Orne asserts that there is no way that even an experienced hypnotist can tell what is true and what is invented in an account elicited under hypnosis. He also warns that an account may become littered with "pseudo-memories," and describes an experiment that proves his point.

First the hypnotist establishes and verifies that the subject went to sleep, say, at midnight on a particular night and slept through without interruption to, say, 8:00 A.M. Then, after inducing deep hypnosis, the subject is regressed

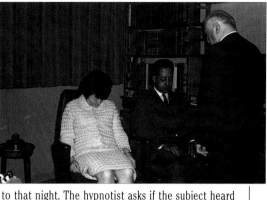

On the couch
Abductees Betty and Barney Hill underwent hypnotic regression in an attempt to discover more about their terrifying experience.

to that night. The hypnotist asks if the subject heard two loud noises (which did not, in fact, occur). The subject will usually say that he or she was awakened by the noises, and if asked to look at the clock by the bed, will give a precise time, say 3:30 A.M.

If the subject is told before coming out of hypnosis to recall that night's events, the pseudo-memory will become as real as an actual event. Later, when fully conscious, the subject will describe hearing loud noises at 3:30 A.M. that night. Orne adds: "The more frequently the subject reports the event, the more firmly established the pseudo-memory will tend to become."

Particularly suspect is testimony elicited by hypnotists with pro-UFO views. Orne comments: "...if the hypnotist has beliefs about what actually occurred, it is exceedingly difficult for him to prevent himself from inadvertently guiding the subject's recall so that [the subject] will eventually 'remember' what he, the hypnotist, believes actually happened."

Ed Walters
This Florida real estate developer managed to take some convincing UFO photographs before his claimed abduction in 1988.

Betty Andreasson
Andreasson's vivid abduction experience seemed to have been colored by her strong Christian fundamentalist faith.

"The Leader"
Barney Hill's sketch of one of the aliens who abducted him, drawn under hypnosis.

---

evidence of extraterrestrial intervention. This growing theoretical split has led to controversy within the UFO field as to the reality of the phenomenon.

Nearly all ufologists, however, would agree that the testimony of the majority of abductees from all over the world is honest and sincere. The abductees certainly believe what they are saying: few have been exposed as hoaxers. Many have undergone psychological testing, and most have been found to be normal. Although in a few cases these accounts of abductions by alien beings can definitely be dismissed as hoaxes or the product of unbalanced minds, most are genuine experiences.

Accurate and honest

But while the reports of the abductees may be accurate and honest, they are not enough. Can these events be objectively verified? What can be held up as evidence?

UFO investigators have searched for physical evidence. Finding some piece of hardware, some effect on the environment, that cannot be explained by any currently known earthly phenomenon, would be strong evidence that the abduction experience was real. Even an independent eyewitness report of a particular incident would be, if not conclusive, strongly persuasive.

Photographic evidence

A great deal of the evidence submitted by UFO researchers has been photographic. Thousands of UFO photographs exist (many of dubious authenticity), but few of them relate to abduction cases. The reasons are pretty clear: abductions tend to happen unexpectedly to people who are unprepared for them. Most reported abductions take place at night — just the time when people are least likely to have a camera with them.

Franck Fontaine
This French abductee reappeared near the site of his abduction a week after he vanished.

♦ PAGE 84

CASEBOOK
ANTONIO VILLAS BOAS

Then, through a hidden door that appeared in the wall of the compartment, came a naked woman.

ANTONIO VILLAS BOAS WAS plowing the fields of the family farm in Minas Gerais, Brazil, during the night of October 15, 1957, when he saw a brightly lit object come down from the sky and land in a field nearby. It was, he said, the third time he had seen a UFO that week — but now the craft's occupants were not content merely to watch him; apparently they wanted to kidnap him.

When the craft landed, Villas Boas first tried to escape on his tractor. The engine stalled and would not restart, so he jumped off and fled on foot. Five aliens chased and captured him. They grabbed his arms and hauled him into their egg-shaped craft.

A blood sample
His captors wore tight-fitting metallic suits, he said, and helmets with narrow visors. They were intent on examining him. Villas Boas was dragged into a circular compartment, where he was held down while a blood sample was taken from his chin. Then he was stripped naked and taken to another compartment, which contained a white plastic-like couch. The alien creatures laid him on the couch and began to wash him with a sponge soaked in a clear, odorless liquid.

Choking gray smoke
Villas Boas was left alone in the room. Gray smoke billowed out of vents in the wall, choking him, until he vomited. Then, through a hidden door that opened in the wall of the compartment, came a naked woman. She looked very human, he said, but was only about 4 feet 9 inches tall.

Villas Boas claimed that he and the alien woman were intimate for some time. Before she left she pointed to her stomach, then to him, then upwards. Villas Boas understood that he had impregnated her, and later professed indignation at being used as "a stallion to improve someone else's stock." After the woman left, his two original captors returned with his clothes and he was allowed to get dressed.

A souvenir from space
Villas Boas was then given a conducted tour of the interior of the craft, where he saw other creatures similar to those who had captured him. He tried to remove a small square box with a clocklike dial on it, as proof of his adventure. One of the craft's occupants, however, angrily snatched it from him. (This is one of the very few cases on record of an abductee attempting to take a piece of hardware from inside an alien spacecraft.)

Eventually Villas Boas was released. The space vehicle took off, becoming brighter during lift-off, then disappearing with a great burst of speed. In the weeks after his experience, small wounds on his hands turned purple and scarred over. He also developed symptoms that the investigator who studied the case, Dr. Olavo Fontes, compared to radiation sickness. However, these same symptoms can indicate other, often psychosomatic, illnesses. There is therefore no conclusive proof that Antonio Villas Boas really did have a close encounter of the third kind.

CASEBOOK
BETTY ANDREASSON

Four small creatures entered the room, passing straight through a wooden door.

BETTY ANDREASSON'S account of her abduction on January 25, 1967, helped to establish the pattern of the classic UFO abduction experience.

In 1967, while her husband was in a hospital recovering from a car crash, Betty was sitting with her seven children and her parents in her house in South Ashburnham, Massachusetts, when a light appeared outside the window. As she later recounted, the rest of her family appeared to go into a state of suspended animation. Four small creatures entered the room, passing straight through a wooden door. They resembled some of the other creatures reported by abductees, with large heads, no noses, small slit-like mouths, and large, almond-shaped "wraparound" eyes. They also wore uniforms with an eagle insignia.

This was all that Betty remembered of the abduction until 1974, when she wrote to a tabloid newspaper about the experience. Eventually her story reached UFO investigator Raymond Fowler. In 1977 she underwent hypnotic regression and produced the following account of her experience.

A physical examination

After the four aliens had entered Betty's house, one of them communicated telepathically with her and led her outside, where an oval-shaped craft was waiting. On board she was subjected to a painful physical examination. A probe was pushed up her nose. She reported: "I heard something break, like a membrane or a veil or something, like a piece of tissue they broke through." Another probe was inserted in her navel, and she was told she was being "measured for procreation."

Next she was made to sit in a glass chair, where she was enclosed by a transparent cover and immersed in fluid; she could breathe through tubes attached to her mouth and nose. A sweet liquid oozed into her mouth. When she was released from the chair, she found that she had traveled to the aliens' planet. Two of the creatures took her along a tunnel and through a series of chambers. The first was full of small reptile-like creatures; the second was a large green-colored space, where they floated over pyramids to a city of mysterious crystalline forms.

Finally she was taken into one of the crystal shapes, where she was confronted by a giant bird that burst into light and then collapsed into a pile of embers. A voice told her that she had been chosen for a special mission, which would be revealed to her. When Betty replied that she believed in God, the voice told her that that was why she had been chosen.

Suspended animation

Betty and her two "guides" returned to the first chamber, and she was again made to sit in the glass chair and taste the sweet fluid. Here, the figure who appeared to be the leader of the extraterrestrials, whose name was Quazgaa, told her that "secrets had been locked in her mind." Two other creatures then escorted her back to her home, where she saw the rest of her family still in a state of suspended animation. The aliens put the family to bed. In the morning they remembered little of this strange encounter.

83

Philip J. Klass

ABDUCTION – FACT OR FANTASY?
In his book *UFO Abductions – A Dangerous Game*, Philip J. Klass reinforces his reputation as the world's leading UFO skeptic. He is deeply suspicious of the use of hypnosis to establish the reality of an abduction experience, and cites in his support experiments conducted by Dr. Robert A. Baker, a professor of psychology at the University of Kentucky.

Dr. Baker subjected several hundred volunteers to hypnosis, and asked them details about their "past and future lives." Baker said that "some of these...lives were quite dramatic, while others were dull and prosaic, depending upon the personality of the subject [and] his or her interest in science-fiction...."

A Martian bartender
Research cited by Dr. Baker suggests that possibly 4 percent of the population is fantasy-prone, and it was these people who gave the best performances. One man took on a different role each week, ranging from a London prostitute to a Roman soldier. Another subject became a bartender in a human colony on Mars in the 22nd century.

Klass's point in citing this evidence is that UFO abduction stories are no different from many other accounts elicited under hypnosis. The stories are told dramatically, with a wealth of detail and great conviction. None has more than a passing relationship to actual events.

Some researchers have treated the physical effects on the witnesses themselves as proof of the reality of their reported experiences. Close encounter witnesses and abductees have displayed a variety of physical symptoms, including nausea, rashes, and discoloration of the skin, as well as sore eyes and glaucoma.

Radiation sickness
These are often the symptoms of radiation sickness, and may have resulted from exposure to high level radiation. They are also the symptoms of

---

The majority of cases on record involve just one person, or a closely related couple, usually husband and wife.

---

a variety of nervous and psychosomatic conditions. Although such symptoms may be strong evidence that something upsetting and traumatic has happened to the witness, they do not prove that a person has been abducted.

One feature that many abductees have in common is that they find a small scar on their bodies after the event. There is a theory that these are the result of tissue sampling by aliens. The fact is that most people have a variety of small scars and marks on their bodies, caused by any number of mishaps from early childhood onwards. Quite apart from this, the gathering of tissue samples by actually cutting small pieces from a subject's body is a remarkably primitive technique for a species apparently advanced enough to be piloting

interplanetary craft. Even present-day medical science can discover a great deal about a body by a swab from inside the mouth, and can take tissue samples without leaving any scar at all.

Independent witnesses
Have any of the abductions been witnessed by anyone, apart from the abductees themselves? Witnesses would certainly help to verify that an abduction had occurred. In fact the majority of cases on record involve just one person, or a closely related couple, usually husband and wife. There must always be an element of doubt in such cases, as investigators can never be sure just how much collusion – and it could easily be subconscious collusion – there might be.

Abduction experiences could also be confirmed if some piece of information about the event is known by two people who otherwise would have no way of colluding. In a way, most of the abduction reports provide this evidence. The accounts of abductions throughout the world are often remarkably similar. Some researchers argue that most if not

Travis Walton
The abductee attempts to defend himself in this illustration from the book The Walton Experience. *This case of a young forestry worker who disappeared in 1975 is often represented as a well-witnessed example. However, the UFO skeptic Philip J. Klass has pointed out a number of flaws in the evidence that suggest that this episode may have been a hoax..*

all of these similarities come not from a shared abduction experience, but from the images of society that we all share — images provided by films, science fiction, and technology.

An abduction blueprint

However, the abduction researcher Budd Hopkins and his colleagues claim that there are a number of very specific and precise pieces of information that have been reported by several quite independent sources — pieces of information so detailed that they could not possibly come from generalized background imagery. In order to preserve the integrity of this information, and to prevent its possible use by hoaxers, the researchers concerned are not prepared to publish details. Naturally, until this is done it is impossible to make any judgment on their claims.

The phenomenon of reported abductions by UFO's is over 30 years old. The cumulation of evidence leads to the inescapable conclusion that the

abduction experience itself is real. Something genuinely strange and disturbing has happened to a large number of people. Witness and abductee testimony alone is sufficient to confirm this. But there is an almost total lack of any objective evidence — physical, photographic, or from independent witnesses — that would confirm that what is happening is a physical abduction by solid creatures piloting solid craft. Despite the vivid reports of the abductees themselves, there can be no final verdict — yet.

Inside the human brain
Modern medicine has come up with a number of techniques that make it a relatively simple matter to search for implants in the brain. This false-color nuclear magnetic resonance image shows a normal human brain.

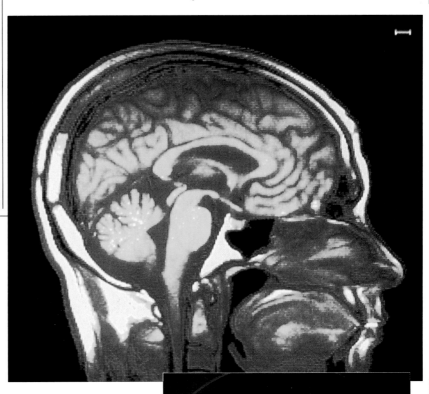

ALIEN IMPLANTS

One night Whitley Strieber, the author and abductee, was awakened by the sensation of a small object being inserted deep into one nostril. Later that night he experienced a feeling he described as a "crunch" behind the bridge of his nose, which was followed by a small nosebleed.

Strieber's story is one that abduction researcher Budd Hopkins has heard on many previous occasions. Hopkins claims that the abductees are being "tagged" with tracking devices that may have a monitoring function. An increasingly common feature of abduction reports is that in addition to undergoing a thorough physical examination, abductees say that a long, thin needle is injected into them. Sometimes this needle is topped with a tiny metal ball, less than one-tenth of an inch in diameter. When the needle is removed, the ball is no longer there. Abductees claim that it has been placed in their nose, ear, or even in their eye socket. Some abductees have reported that a small ball has been removed from their bodies during a similar operation.

A distressing memory

The memory of this procedure has often distressed the abductee, and many people have undergone brain scans in the hope of revealing the presence of an implant. The results have been inconclusive. Some anomalies have shown up, but it is not clear whether these are natural, or the result of technical malfunctions, or signs of a foreign body.

In September, 1986, the well-respected science journal *Nature* published a report by gynecologists at a hospital in Oxford, England. They had found a mysterious object in a woman's amniotic fluid during a routine prenatal chromosome test. This object was made of an unknown material and consisted of small dots in a regular grid pattern; it measured only 10 microns, which was considerably smaller than the size of any other reported implants.

No one has yet explained satisfactorily what this strange object is; on the other hand, there is no evidence to suggest that it is an alien implant. More and better physical evidence of this type will be needed to convince the scientific community of the reality of visiting aliens.

CT scanner
A computed tomography scanning machine that could be used to search for implants by taking cross-sectional X-rays of the brain.

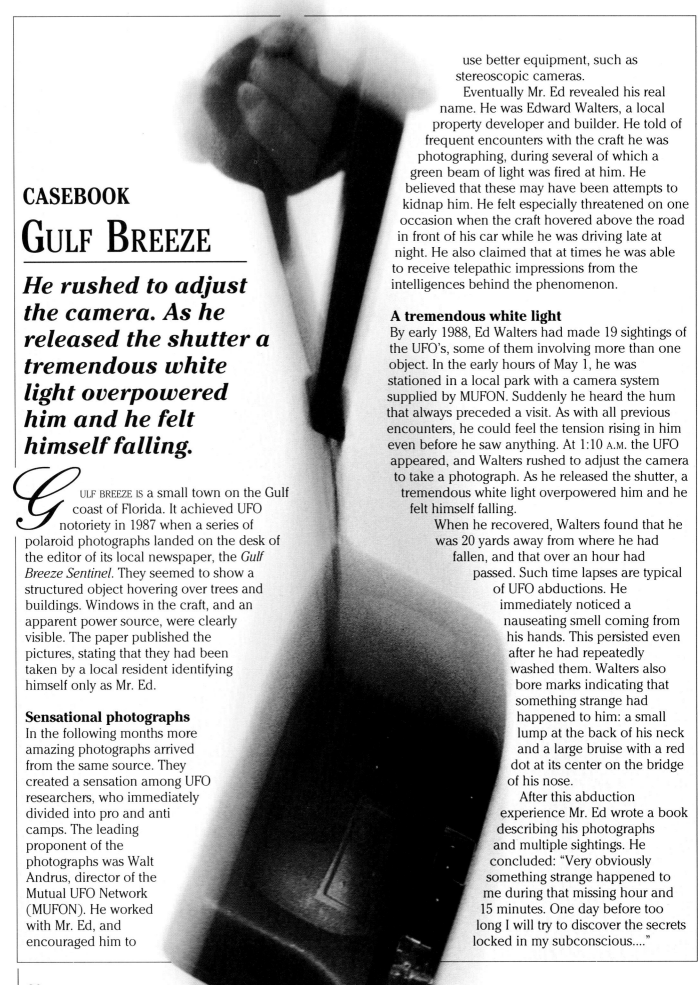

CASEBOOK
GULF BREEZE

He rushed to adjust the camera. As he released the shutter a tremendous white light overpowered him and he felt himself falling.

G ULF BREEZE IS a small town on the Gulf coast of Florida. It achieved UFO notoriety in 1987 when a series of polaroid photographs landed on the desk of the editor of its local newspaper, the *Gulf Breeze Sentinel*. They seemed to show a structured object hovering over trees and buildings. Windows in the craft, and an apparent power source, were clearly visible. The paper published the pictures, stating that they had been taken by a local resident identifying himself only as Mr. Ed.

Sensational photographs
In the following months more amazing photographs arrived from the same source. They created a sensation among UFO researchers, who immediately divided into pro and anti camps. The leading proponent of the photographs was Walt Andrus, director of the Mutual UFO Network (MUFON). He worked with Mr. Ed, and encouraged him to use better equipment, such as stereoscopic cameras.

Eventually Mr. Ed revealed his real name. He was Edward Walters, a local property developer and builder. He told of frequent encounters with the craft he was photographing, during several of which a green beam of light was fired at him. He believed that these may have been attempts to kidnap him. He felt especially threatened on one occasion when the craft hovered above the road in front of his car while he was driving late at night. He also claimed that at times he was able to receive telepathic impressions from the intelligences behind the phenomenon.

A tremendous white light
By early 1988, Ed Walters had made 19 sightings of the UFO's, some of them involving more than one object. In the early hours of May 1, he was stationed in a local park with a camera system supplied by MUFON. Suddenly he heard the hum that always preceded a visit. As with all previous encounters, he could feel the tension rising in him even before he saw anything. At 1:10 A.M. the UFO appeared, and Walters rushed to adjust the camera to take a photograph. As he released the shutter, a tremendous white light overpowered him and he felt himself falling.

When he recovered, Walters found that he was 20 yards away from where he had fallen, and that over an hour had passed. Such time lapses are typical of UFO abductions. He immediately noticed a nauseating smell coming from his hands. This persisted even after he had repeatedly washed them. Walters also bore marks indicating that something strange had happened to him: a small lump at the back of his neck and a large bruise with a red dot at its center on the bridge of his nose.

After this abduction experience Mr. Ed wrote a book describing his photographs and multiple sightings. He concluded: "Very obviously something strange happened to me during that missing hour and 15 minutes. One day before too long I will try to discover the secrets locked in my subconscious...."

BETTY AND BARNEY HILL

They reported meeting humanoid creatures with large "wraparound" eyes, no noses, and mouths with no lips.

THE ABDUCTION OF Betty and Barney Hill on September 19, 1961, is one of the earliest cases to be reported. It has been the subject of at least one full-length book and was dramatized in a made-for-TV movie. It has also provided a framework for many subsequent abduction tales, with its themes of missing time, medical examination, and investigation by hypnotic regression.

A light in the sky

The Hills were driving through the White Mountains toward their home in Portsmouth, New Hampshire, after a holiday in Canada, when they became aware of a light in the sky that was apparently following their car. They stopped to look at it through binoculars, and it appeared as a curved band of light. Barney saw windows in the shape, with figures wearing uniforms moving about behind them. At first he thought the object was a military helicopter. As it moved closer, Barney continued to observe it through his binoculars until eventually he panicked. He felt that he was about to be captured — he described one of the crewmen as looking like a Nazi. He leapt back into the car, and he and his wife drove home.

Alien nightmares

In the next few days Betty began having nightmares in which she and Barney were taken aboard a disc-shaped craft and examined by aliens. Barney began suffering increasingly from stress, and a ring of warts developed on his groin. When Barney tried to reconstruct the events of their journey, he realized that their drive through New Hampshire had taken two hours longer than normal.

Barney's increasing anxiety led him to seek psychiatric help. Eventually, at his own suggestion, a Boston psychiatrist, Dr. Benjamin Simon, was called in to regress him to the encounter episode.

The hypnotic regressions began to reveal details of the period of missing time. Barney's and Betty's recollections were recorded separately, but their stories closely tallied. They reported meeting humanoid creatures with large "wraparound" eyes, no noses, and mouths that seemed to be a mere slit, with no lips.

Both husband and wife gave accounts of medical examinations: Barney's included a cuplike instrument that was put round his genitals, and Betty reported a long needle being inserted into her navel. Some UFO investigators interpreted these as sperm and pregnancy tests. Betty was shown a screen with a map on it — a series of dots depicting the star system from which the aliens originated. Betty was later able to reproduce this from memory. Her sketch corresponded closely to the view of our sun and the neighboring stars from a few light-years beyond the Zeta Reticuli star system.

Psychological tensions

Dr. Simon concluded that the case was a subconscious fantasy originating in psychological tensions in the couple. He thought it significant that they were a mixed-race couple — Betty was white, Barney black — and that this may have contributed to the stress in their relationship. Barney died in 1969, aged 46, of a cerebral hemorrhage. Betty continued to be interested in UFO's. She claimed to have seen many thousands more since her abduction, and to be able to communicate with them telepathically.

CASEBOOK
CERGY-PONTOISE

Few people could produce any witnesses of their abduction by aliens, but Franck Fontaine had two.

The witnesses
Franck Fontaine (left), who claims he was abducted by aliens, revisits the site with the two friends who reported his disappearance, Jean-Pierre Prévost and Salomon N'Diaye.

AT CERGY-PONTOISE near Paris, France, Franck Fontaine was reported to have been snatched by a UFO in the early hours of November 26, 1979, while helping his friends Jean-Pierre Prévost and Salomon N'Diaye load a station wagon with clothes for an outdoor market. Though the two friends did not actually see Fontaine being taken, they had observed a UFO a few minutes earlier; they saw a great ball of light surround the car in which he was sitting; they saw a beam shoot up into the sky from the vehicle; and when they ran to the car, they could find no trace of their friend. The conclusion was inescapable: Fontaine had been taken by aliens.

The missing week
Distraught, his friends went straight to the police. (The fact that they did so, considering that they had been driving their car without a license, helped persuade many of their sincerity.) When the press heard of the affair, the news spread around the world. The head of the local police told the media that he knew of no grounds for disbelieving the young men's story. Jimmy Guieu, author of two bestselling books on flying saucers, also believed their story without hesitation.

For a week, speculation was rife. Then Fontaine returned, and the case made even bigger headlines. "Frenchman back to earth with a bump!" wrote *The Times* of London.

Fontaine told the police and the press how he had woken to find himself lying in a cabbage field close to the road where he had been abducted. He walked to the nearby apartment building to call on his friends, who were amazed to see him. Only then did Fontaine learn that he had been gone for a week.

No memories at all
At first, he had no memories at all of what had happened to him during the previous week, thinking that he had simply fallen asleep for half an hour. Little by little, however, confused images of being aboard a spacecraft began to come back to him. Guieu's research group, the impressively named World Institute for Scientific Advancement, offered to hypnotize Fontaine to restore his lapsed memory, but he refused. Instead, his friend Jean-Pierre Prévost volunteered. Under hypnosis, the aliens spoke through Prévost. They said that they had chosen Prévost, not Fontaine, to be their spokesman on earth. Fontaine's abduction had simply been a device to establish contact.

Within a few weeks Guieu published a bestselling book on the subject, and later in the year, Prévost

Awaiting aliens
In the summer of 1980, a group of UFO enthusiasts waited ior days in a field in Cergy-Pontoise, hoping to meet the space people who had allegedly abducted Fontaine the previous year.

UFO believer
Jimmy Guieu — UFO enthusiast and author of more than 20 science fiction titles — never wavered in his belief that Fontaine had been abducted aboard a spacecraft.

wrote his own account, *La vérité sur l'affaire de Cergy-Pontoise (The Truth About the Cergy-Pontoise Affair)*.

In August 1980, Prévost arranged an open meeting with the aliens at the scene of the abduction, and a crowd of believers gathered to greet them when they landed. Unfortunately, the aliens did not arrive. The believers were not too discouraged, however, and

---

Prévost arranged an open meeting with the aliens at the scene of the abduction.

Prévost went on to form an association with its own journal, radio network, and plans for annual gatherings. A number of young people joined him, but the public lost interest in the affair.

Another big get-together was organized for August 1983, when the extraterrestrials were again expected to show up. A short while before the event, however, Prévost confessed to the press that it had all been a fraud. "The Cergy affair

was a lot of rubbish. We staged the whole thing to get a little money." According to Prévost, Fontaine had not been abducted at all, but had spent a week hiding in a friend's apartment.

Seven-day wonder

That should have been the end of the Cergy-Pontoise case. However, N'Diaye, the second witness, was furious at Prévost's confession. "What we lived through, we really lived through! Jean-Pierre can't just wipe out the episode from our lives with his lies. I don't know what he hopes to gain by it. Where he claims he hid Franck exists only in his own imagination."

Fontaine himself was equally indignant. "The guy is crazy! I can't imagine what he hopes to gain by spinning such a yarn. It wasn't enough for him, all the trouble we had telling the truth: now he goes nuts and pretends he made up the whole thing! It makes you sick! He had no right to do such a thing...."

Guieu, who reports these responses in his 1986 book *Le monde étrange des contactes (The Strange World of the Contactees)*, is as convinced as ever that the original story is the truth. He has nothing but scorn for Prévost and for the researchers who pick holes in the young men's account. There is no doubt in his mind that extraterrestrials did indeed abduct Franck Fontaine that winter morning at Cergy-Pontoise.

Sci-Fi at the Movies

The Early Days

The first sci-fi movie was Journey on the Moon in 1902. Fifty years later, the genre was at its peak, reflecting and influencing our perception of extraterrestrials.

The Day of the Triffids (1963)

The publicity posters for this classic invasion movie promised spine-chilling terror. This time the terrifying threat from outer space comes through plant spores. These arrive in a wonderful meteorite storm, blinding all who observe the spectacle and mutating harmless plants into vicious alien killers called Triffids. The scene is set for the traditional battle between Them and Us.

THE 1950's WERE THE golden decade of science fiction films. This was the age of incredible plots, evil aliens, dramatic dialogue, and wonderful overacting. The sighting of the first flying saucer in 1947, and an apprehension about atomic weapons, led people to fear the possible existence of beings from other worlds. Movie-makers were quick to exploit the public's interest, and rapidly produced numerous low-budget, black-and-white films. Cold war paranoia and the communist witch-hunts of the period simply added to the widespread terror of being taken over by aliens and increased the public appetite for science fiction.

It Came From Outer Space (1953)

An astronomer investigates the crash landing of a meteor in the Arizona desert and finds an alien spaceship. The shapeless one-eyed monsters that emerge from the craft terrify the local inhabitants, but the scientist is not sure that they mean us harm.

FANTASTIC SIGHTS LEAP AT YOU!
IN 3-DIMENSION
AMAZING! EXCITING! SPECTACULAR!

IT CAME FROM OUTER SPACE

Richard CARLSON · Barbara RUSH
with CHARLES DRAKE · RUSSELL JOHNSON
KATHLEEN HUGHES · JOE SAWYER

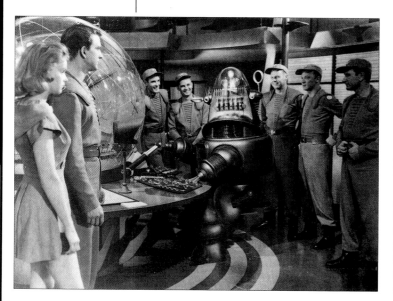

Forbidden Planet (1956)

Based loosely on William Shakespeare's play *The Tempest*, the action takes place on the planet Altair-4. Human castaways discover underground storage chambers that hold the knowledge of an extinct alien race. The narrative warns humankind against the misuse of power. But this worthy message was generally overlooked by the moviegoing public, and the success of the film was due largely to its metallic star, Robby the Robot.

The War of the Worlds (1953)
H.G. Wells's novel, *The War of the Worlds*, describing the invasion of earth by armies of rampaging Martians, provided the perfect plot for the 1950's. It played on all the fears of a paranoid public in the middle of the cold war: the aliens were hostile, powerful, and right here on earth.

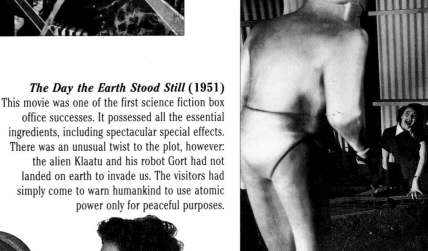

Man From Planet X (1951)
In many ways this is a typical low-budget science fiction film. But for perhaps the first time the alien is not depicted as a terrifying invader, but as being weak and vulnerable.

The Day the Earth Stood Still (1951)
This movie was one of the first science fiction box office successes. It possessed all the essential ingredients, including spectacular special effects. There was an unusual twist to the plot, however: the alien Klaatu and his robot Gort had not landed on earth to invade us. The visitors had simply come to warn humankind to use atomic power only for peaceful purposes.

This Island Earth (1955)
This movie is a rehash of the sci-fi stories that were churned out in their thousands in the popular magazines of the 1930's and 1940's. The nonsensical plot involves grotesque aliens who have mastered space travel and possess many strange gadgets and weapons. Yet we have superior knowledge, and the aliens' plan is to kidnap human scientists to save their own doomed planet of Metaluna.

THE MODERN ERA

Science fiction has come a long way. There is not much to link the popular, imaginative sci-fi comics of the 1930's and 1940's, and the delightful earthbound movie dramas of the 1950's, with today's action-packed space blockbusters.

*M*AN'S FIRST STEPS on the moon were taken on July 21, 1969, by Neil Armstrong. This dramatic event fired the public imagination and proved to be a watershed in the development of the science fiction genre. Space had been conquered, and fears for the future had receded; whatever the problem, humankind could solve it. Gone were the invading hordes of warlike aliens; the movies now reflected the scientific optimism of the period.

At the same time, the genre lost a sense of wonder and mystery. It may have been in an effort to replace this that bizarre, but in some cases approachable space creatures and robots were increasingly introduced into plots. They added spice to the new generation of high-tech, high-budget adventure movies about the frontiers of space.

The Blob (1989)
In a remake of the 1958 movie, this potentially interesting story of an alien creature that can change shape is once again transformed into a monster-on-the-loose movie. The motives and intelligence of the creature are not explored, and the fact that it is not a native of this earth is almost irrelevant.

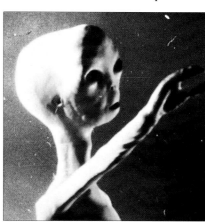

Close Encounters of the Third Kind (1977)
Of all the dozens of science fiction movies, this is the one that most strongly reflects actual abductee cases. The film tracks the increasingly bizarre behavior of apparently normal people who find themselves being drawn toward a strangely shaped hill in Wyoming, known as the Devil's Tower. The eventual arrival of the alien craft, in the closing moments of the movie, is one of the most emotionally powerful sequences ever to be filmed. The box office success of *Close Encounters* demonstrates how many people long to believe that there are benevolent beings in the sky.

2001 – A Space Odyssey (1968)

Stanley Kubrick launched on an unsuspecting world the first of the new generation of sci-fi films. The burgeoning space program had excited the public and made it receptive to fantastic futuristic movies. The film neatly combines the fears of the past with optimism for the future. HAL, the computer on board the spacecraft, goes out of control and kills all but one of the human crew. But the ending is hopeful: humankind is reborn once more.

Alien (1979)

This is a classic suspense movie. A hideous alien creature is accidentally brought on board the starship when the crew investigate an apparently abandoned alien craft. It lurks in the recesses of their ship. The first glimpse of the creature is truly memorable. It bursts out of the torso of one of the crew members just as they are all sitting down to eat.

The Thing (1982)

The distinction between science fiction and horror becomes blurred in this movie. The 1951 version of *The Thing* closed with the classic line "watch the skies!" playing on the paranoia of its audience in that decade. But the modern remake relied heavily on the revolting appearance and violent behavior of a creature that had been accidentally released from the frozen Arctic wastes.

E.T. The Extraterrestrial (1982)

This film does not rely for its effect on technical gadgetry and gleaming spacecraft. The awe-inspiring aspects of sci-fi are replaced by a celebration of innocence. The boy hero, Thomas Elliott, wants to protect a helpless young alien whose only wish is to go home. As Thomas rescues, befriends, and finally saves E.T., the director, Steven Spielberg, moves us through a whole range of emotions. The climax of the film is the now-legendary magical BMX bike ride.

THE ALIENS

Some people argue that the aliens come from planets in other solar systems; others claim that they emerge from black holes in space, from a parallel universe, or even from inside the earth itself.

HEN CLOSE ENCOUNTERS were first reported in the 1950's, it was easy for the contactees to believe that the beings whom they met came from other worlds. When Aura Rhanes told Truman Bethurum that she was from the planet Clarion, nobody could categorically deny it. Nor could anyone contradict Howard Menger when he said that he had encountered friendly space people who told him they came from the moon.

Scientists had yet to establish that there was no intelligent life apart from ourselves in our solar system. That knowledge only came with the space exploration of the 1960's. Space probes revealed, for example, that Venus (much favored by contactees as a planet from which aliens traveled to earth) had an atmosphere as hot as that inside a pressure cooker.

Other solar systems

Sometimes contactees claimed that they had met aliens from planets in other solar systems. As these planets could be anywhere in our universe, it was impossible to disprove their existence. Even when their location was precisely described — such as Zeta Reticuli, home of Betty and Barney Hills' alleged abductors — they were too far from earth for scientists to confirm their existence, let alone prove if they could sustain life.

Astronomer Carl Sagan believes it is not inconceivable that there may be planets that could sustain intelligent life in other galaxies. Vast distances, however, separate us from such planets. To give some idea of the distances involved, the stellar constellation that lies nearest to earth, Alpha Centauri, is over four light years away. Even using the fastest craft yet constructed, it would still take 80,000 years to reach it.

The extraterrestrial hypothesis

The most popular explanation of the UFO enigma has been the extraterrestrial hypothesis (ETH). This holds that UFO's are craft piloted by aliens who travel through space and/or time.

If alien spacecraft are visiting our planet, then it is conceivable that their occupants should explore it. A natural development from this is that the aliens should next turn their attention to earth's inhabitants. Thus the ETH conveniently explains the sudden emergence of the abduction phenomenon.

However, this thesis does not explain the variety of the types of aliens reported. Nor does it explain why, if

BLACK HOLES

A black hole is formed when a massive star collapses. As the star dies, its core becomes denser and denser, causing it to collapse under its own gravitational pull. Eventually, all the star's matter vanishes into a swirling black hole whose gravity is so powerful that not even light can escape from it. Astronomers have known of the existence of black holes for many years, but it is only recently that they have actually located one.

Distant galaxies

Some astronomers believe that black holes are doorways into distant galaxies and, possibly, the past and the future. Some astronomers speculate that black holes could be shortcuts for travelers through time and space. Astronomer Carl Sagan conjures up the image of what he calls "a black hole rapid-transit system."

Ufologists have used the idea of black holes to explain how extraterrestrial craft could travel the vast distances from one star system to another. It is a fact that matter can pass through these holes out of our time-space continuum. Presumably, ufologists argue, matter can enter through them; in that case, so, in theory, could an alien spacecraft.

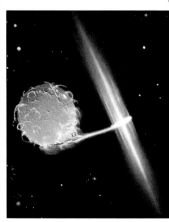

Star guzzler
In this artist's impression, star matter is sucked into a black hole by the collapsing star's relentless gravitational pull. Some ufologists believe that a black hole is the doorway into a new dimension.

Alien gaze
In recent years, descriptions of their captors by American abductees have displayed an unnerving similarity. Aliens are described as having huge, dark, empty wells for eyes, in which the terrified abductees felt they were being swallowed up.

MYSTERIOUS MUTILATORS

An Appaloosa gelding called Snippy from Alamosa, Colorado, met with a gruesome fate in 1967. Its carcass was found with all the flesh neatly removed from its head and neck.

Snippy's death set the pattern for a series of bizarre animal mutilations that have occurred across the U.S.A. In all cases, parts of the bodies were removed, such as the eyes, ears, genitals, or anus.

UFO experiments

Some people have claimed that the mutilations are the result of experiments conducted by UFO-borne aliens. Others suspect that Satanic cults are using animals in their rituals. Another theory is that cattle are being used in secret U.S. government experiments involving chemical and germ warfare. However, the skeptics and the ranchers seem to favor the theory that these animals have been mutilated by natural predators, such as wolves or coyotes.

Snippy's demise
Snippy's radiation levels were tested but revealed nothing unusual. An autopsy failed to establish the cause of death.

the aliens originated from other solar systems, they would necessarily be humanoid in appearance — which is how the majority of witnesses describe them. Furthermore, visitors from other worlds would probably not be able to survive in our atmosphere; the aliens are usually described as being without any obvious breathing apparatus.

UFO investigators worldwide concluded that the ETH just could not explain the variety and the extent of the UFO experience. European researchers, such as Frenchman Bertrand Méheust, tend to explain UFO's in terms of the expression of the witness's psychological processes. He believes that the images produced by these workings are conditioned by the society in which the witness lives.

However, in America many leading UFO investigators still use the ETH as the basis of all their research. Today these investigators are far less specific about the origins of the extraterrestrials than the earlier ufologists were.

Interplanetary arks

Some investigators who have remained convinced that UFO's are extraterrestrial craft have suggested that UFO's originate from large interplanetary arks. These giant spacecraft, they claim, were built by the aliens and launched from the home planet when it faced destruction.

Martian wars?
Late 19th-century observers reported seeing warlike activity on Mars. Photographs taken by the Viking 1 orbiter showed this to be nothing but dust clouds.

Contactees often told how the "space brothers" they encountered warned that if we earthdwellers did not mend our ways, we would destroy our planet. Sometimes they said that their own planet had been destroyed. Arthur C. Clarke, author of the science fiction classic *2001 — A Space Odyssey*, has suggested that the building of such arks is a project toward which our technology should strive, as humankind might one day have need of such a craft.

Many alien species

However appealing this idea is to some, there are problems if this theory is supposed to explain the variety and sheer number of UFO's that have been reported since the 1950's. If all the aliens originate from one such ark, then this craft would be inhabited by many species of alien, at varying stages of physical, technological, and spiritual development. This seems unlikely. The idea that there are a large number of

> **Some investigators have suggested that UFO's originate from large interplanetary arks.**

such arks orbiting in the vicinity of earth seems just as unlikely. This theory can be dismissed as the product of the vivid imagination of science fiction writers.

Hyperspace

By the 1970's the ETH began to lose its place as the main theory that explained where the UFO's came from. Many adherents of the ETH acknowledged what space exploration had revealed, that no other planet in our solar system could support intelligent life. If UFO's were alien craft, they must come from other solar systems.

Such a hypothesis immediately raised the question of how these alien craft could travel the vast distances from one solar system to another. In theory, this could be done if the extraterrestrial travelers circumvented the limitations of time and space as we know them by traveling through hyperspace.

A fourth dimension

The central idea is that holes exist within our time-space continuum through which matter can enter or exit from hyperspace. A craft may "drop out" of space at one point and reappear at another position thousands, or even millions, of light-years away. For this to be possible, a fourth dimension must exist through which a spacecraft can take shortcuts inaccessible in a three-

Martian view
The Mars Viking *unmanned probe transmitted photographs from Mars in 1980.*

dimensional world. Proponents of this theory believe that black holes are the doorways into this fourth dimension.

Alternative realities

In the late 1960's the American ufologist Alan Greenfield introduced the idea of alternative realities to explain the origin of the aliens. He suggested that they were not from another planet but from another dimension, which co-exists with our own world but is normally hidden from us. From time to time, however, these different worlds interact, and this is what causes such anomalies as UFO's, alien beings, and even ghosts.

The concept of windows in time and space is not new. It forms the basis of a whole array of mystical theories. It had the advantage of explaining the vague, transitory nature of much of the UFO phenomenon. However, it was never really an option as a serious explanation, being so vague and open-ended that it was impossible to prove or disprove.

What emerges most clearly from alleged alien encounters is the part the human mind plays in the whole equation. There is virtually no physical evidence to suggest that the aliens whom the witnesses, contactees, and abductees have met actually come from other worlds. There is much more to suggest that the alien visitors spring from deep within the recesses of the human mind.

HOLLOW EARTH ALIENS

Some people have claimed that the "aliens" are from our own world, coming either from remote and inhospitable parts of the planet, or indeed from beneath its surface. This idea first appeared in print in the 1940's, in a science fiction magazine called *Amazing Stories*, that was edited by pioneer ufologist Ray Palmer.

Robert Shaver, a contributor to the magazine, alleged that members of a non-human race — the Dero — lived in a series of giant caverns across the world. He said that the Dero were able, with the aid of machines, to affect events adversely, such as causing storms on the surface of the planet. Shaver's ideas touched a chord with many of Palmer's readers, thousands of whom wrote to confirm these tales.

Bright Venus
The Pioneer-Venus *orbiter photographed Venus in 1978. The photographs showed that Venus's cloudy, turbulent atmosphere could not support intelligent life.*

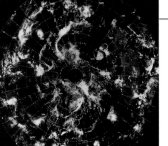

Polar hole
The photograph, taken from space, that confused Hollow Earthers.

Another theory from the 1940's suggested that the earth is a hollow sphere within which an entire civilization has developed. Flying craft from the earth's center make occasional visits to our world, entering and exiting through large holes at the North and South Poles.

Photographs from space

Photographs taken in 1967 by the *ESSA-5* reconnaissance satellite showed black voids at the North and South Poles that the supporters of the Hollow Earth theory took as conclusive proof. What they actually showed was the blank space where the camera was unable to produce an image because of the path of its orbit.

SPACE PARADE

Eyewitnesses report a number of different types of alien visitors; in fact, they vary in almost every imaginable way.

THERE HAVE BEEN REPORTS of space creatures for centuries, but the numbers of sightings seem to have increased dramatically since the first flying saucers were seen in the late 1940's. And the aliens come in a baffling variety of shapes and sizes.

Surprisingly, however, the aliens themselves are not so very different from human beings — most have two arms, two legs, and one head. For this reason some ufologists doubt their existence: surely, they say, visitors from outer space would not look so much like ourselves. Astronomer Carl Sagan, author of *The Cosmic Connection: An Extraterrestrial Perspective*, believes that the aliens sighted so far are "stodgy in their unimaginativeness" and are hence the inhabitants of human minds, not extraterrestrial spaceships. But whatever the experts may say, close encounters of the third kind continue to be reported.

On little cat feet

A glowing alien less than four feet tall appeared to the Sutton family of Hopkinsville, Kentucky, on the night of August 21, 1955. The creature had long arms ending in clawlike hands, a round head, pointed ears, and bulging yellow eyes. This creature and at least one other alien terrorized the Suttons throughout the night.

Hovering creatures

The floating aliens who subjected two Pascagoula, Mississippi, shipyard workers to a physical examination in 1973 were five feet tall with gray, wrinkled skin. The men described them as having long arms ending in mitten-like claws, no necks, straight legs, and round feet. Their faces were terrifyingly blank.

Inhuman relations

The humanoids seen by Antonio Villas Boas on October 15, 1957, were five feet tall and dressed in white body suits. Through their helmets, Villas Boas could glimpse pale blue eyes. Chillingly, the aliens were intent on using Villas Boas to improve their species. His account suggests that even now in a distant galaxy may live a child — half alien, half human — the result of this encounter.

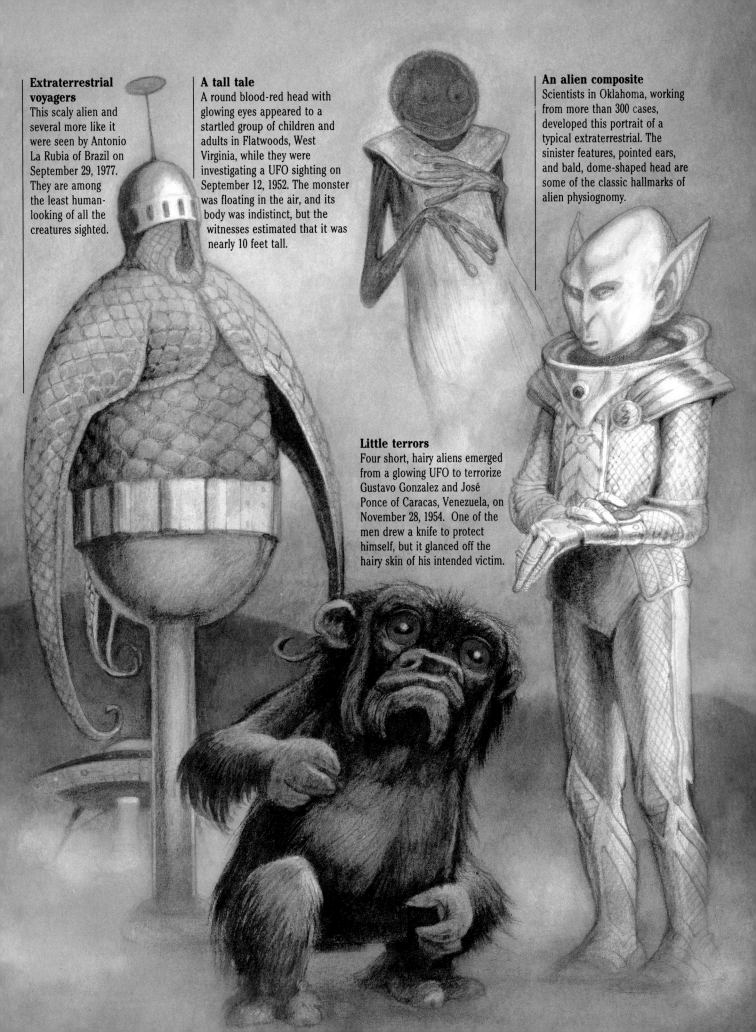

Extraterrestrial voyagers
This scaly alien and several more like it were seen by Antonio La Rubia of Brazil on September 29, 1977. They are among the least human-looking of all the creatures sighted.

A tall tale
A round blood-red head with glowing eyes appeared to a startled group of children and adults in Flatwoods, West Virginia, while they were investigating a UFO sighting on September 12, 1952. The monster was floating in the air, and its body was indistinct, but the witnesses estimated that it was nearly 10 feet tall.

An alien composite
Scientists in Oklahoma, working from more than 300 cases, developed this portrait of a typical extraterrestrial. The sinister features, pointed ears, and bald, dome-shaped head are some of the classic hallmarks of alien physiognomy.

Little terrors
Four short, hairy aliens emerged from a glowing UFO to terrorize Gustavo Gonzalez and José Ponce of Caracas, Venezuela, on November 28, 1954. One of the men drew a knife to protect himself, but it glanced off the hairy skin of his intended victim.

CHAPTER FOUR

FAITH AND PARANOIA

Thousands of ordinary people have reported contact with aliens. The response to this phenomenon varies, from the believers who take it at face value to the skeptics who make strenuous efforts to debunk it. And the faithful believe that the authorities know more than they admit.

There are similarities between reports of UFO abduction and accounts of dreams and nightmares. The way in which they are remembered, the manner in which events seem to happen without particular cause or context, are typically dreamlike. We have seen how little effect, if any, these apparently dramatic happenings have on the broader, physical world beyond the consciousness of the people who are

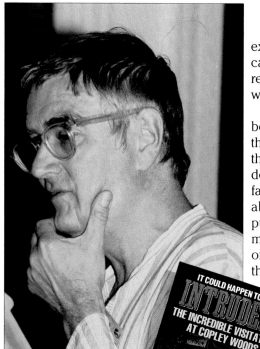

Budd Hopkins
A New York artist who has pioneered abduction research, Hopkins's first book, Missing Time, *was published in 1981. It pinpointed one of the characteristic elements of an abduction experience, a period of time, from several minutes to several hours, that is unaccounted for in the memory of the subject. Hopkins's second book,* Intruders, *was published in 1987. It concentrates on some bizarre case histories that Hopkins discovered by subjecting alleged abductees to hypnotic regression.*

experiencing them. If we cannot accept abductions as real, physical events, then what is going on?

Two lines of argument can be broadly dismissed. First, there is the suggestion that the accounts are hoaxes, deliberately concocted for fame, profit, or both. But few abductees seek direct publicity. Few go to the media, and the majority have only fragmented recall of their experiences before their recollection is assisted by others. If they go public, they are more likely to meet with ridicule than with offers of money. Any individual seeking personal profit would be unwise to seek it this way. Second, there is the implication that the sanity of most abductees is in doubt. The psychiatric evidence so far collected simply does not support this view.

So where do we begin to look for an explanation? It is difficult enough to investigate a report of any unusual nonrepeatable event — the sighting of a light in the sky, or even of a physical craft. In those situations, although you are still only dealing with the memory of an event, it was at least perceived through the conventional senses. If abductions are only perceived internally, in some area of the mind, they are even more difficult to investigate. Particularly if they are for some reason "blocked" — made more difficult to remember by some conscious or unconscious process. The use of hypnotic regression may assist in "unblocking," but it can also lead to confusion, and to the imaginative construction of scenarios that may either satisfy a need in the abductee, or which the abductee believes are what the hypnotist wants to hear.

Researchers do not, however, go and drag passers-by off the street and turn them into abductees. Witnesses write to authors and go to investigators and research organizations because they feel that something strange has happened to them, and they want to know what it was. Their memories are often so real to them as to be disturbing. Most worrying of all, actual marks and scars have been found on the skin of those who believe that they have been physically examined by extraterrestrial beings.

Alienation
Not surprisingly these individuals feel themselves separated from those around them; in the early stages by the sheer strangeness of their experience, but as time and investigation go on, often by more positive emotions. Some abductees become more caring and concerned people as a result of their experiences.

However, there are also negative emotions: anxiety about when the next abduction, examination, or interference will take place; worry about the medical implications of their experiences; fear for the future. These are all sensations that set people apart from the rest of the community, but not from other abductees.

> **Scars have been found on the skin of those who believe that they have been examined by aliens.**

The very barriers that separate the abductees from the rest of us have made the abductee phenomenon into a movement. It is a social grouping that people can become part of by making certain revelations. These groups offer support and care for their members. Despite the geographical distances that divide abductees in America, a nationwide network has developed, made up of people who have been abducted or who believe abductions are taking place.

An artist, Budd Hopkins, set up an abductee support group, like those for addictions, in New York City in the early 1980's. He says: "Our group environment is more party-like than meeting-like....The mood is always one of friendship and ease. At some point in the evening, we usually slip into a more formal mode, with round-robin, one-at-a-time discussions of various issues associated with UFO abductions." These issues include: how to avoid future abductions; how to discuss the subject with children, especially if they too are having abduction experiences; and how to cope with the problems people have in acknowledging and admitting their abductee status to family and friends.

Strieber's alien?
This painting of his captor by an abductee bears an uncanny resemblance to the alien on the cover of Communion.

Media sensations

A number of researchers and hypnotists have given this recounting of experience the framework in which it thrives. And the sensation-hungry media have fed off the accounts, and fueled and encouraged them in turn. The writer Whitley Strieber, himself an abductee, made the experience the basis of a bestselling book and a feature film. Describing the period of his publicity tour for his book *Communion* (published in 1987), Strieber said: "I have been on over 40 live television and radio shows....On these programs I have been before 15 live audiences ranging in size from 50 to 700 persons. I have taken 218 telephone calls on the air. In the past six weeks I have received over 500 letters from *Communion* readers responding to the address in the back of the book....The overwhelming number of letters have been positive. Five have appeared to be from seriously disorganized minds. Most of the letters are as striking for their articulate style as for their astonishing content. Eighty-eight percent of the letters describe some sort of 'visitor' experience. About 40 percent report an actual abduction."

This was only shortly after the publication of *Communion*. Two years later he was still receiving 30 letters a day. Similarly, Hopkins gave a contact address in both his books: *Missing Time* (1981) and *Intruders* (1987). He has worked personally with more than 300 alleged abductees.

There are some important differences in the ways in which Strieber and Hopkins approach their research. Strieber's contacts tend to echo his own experience as an abductee, with similar fears about mind control, the possibility of implants in the brain, and physical scars and damage to the body. Strieber, among others, is also critical of overusing hypnotism to aid in the recall of alleged abductions.

Strieber set up an embryonic support network for abductees, called the Communion Foundation. In the first issue of the *Communion Letter*, Strieber mentioned that the Communion Foundation "is now arranging for witnesses who remember needle intrusions (in their heads) or have strange scars to undergo Magnetic Resonance Imaging scans of the areas where the intrusions took place." His attitude to abduction experiences in general can be ascertained from an advertisement for the *Communion Letter*: "Learn how to respond usefully and effectively to the visitors if they appear in your life. Discover the mystery, the wonder and the beauty of the experience...the things that ordinary media will not reveal...the strange and wonderful truths that are rushing up out of the darkness." Hopkins's Intruders Foundation — and its associated publication, the *IF Bulletin* — takes a different approach. Hopkins has trained as a hypnotist, and himself undertakes hypnosis. He has for some years encouraged informal support and discussion among the abductees known to him. As he

Whitley Strieber
Strieber claimed to have suffered a number of terrifying visitations by aliens at his weekend house in New York state. After undergoing hypnosis and therapy, he wrote a bestselling book about his experiences, which was later made into a film. He took an unusually optimistic view of this strange phenomenon. He wrote that his book, Communion, *is "about forming a new relationship with the unknown...."*

Leo Sprinkle
A professor of psychology at the University of Wyoming, Sprinkle has studied a large number of close encounter witnesses. His theory is that the human race is undergoing a process of education at the hands of benevolent extraterrestrial beings.

says in issue No.1 of the *IF Bulletin*: "You can take comfort in the fact that you are not alone and that there now exists a network of investigators, therapists, hypnotists, and medical personnel to help you. This network is part of IF. There are many other cooperating radiologists, gynecologists, neurosurgeons, and other medical personnel — as well as psychiatrists, psychologists, and therapists who do not carry out regressive hypnosis — located in various towns and cities in the U.S.A. and Canada. All, however, operate under the premise that these seemingly incredible UFO encounters may actually be occurring exactly as described."

Abduction scenarios

For the *IF Bulletin*, abduction is a very serious matter indeed. What Strieber has described as "alien rape" scenarios, with varying degrees of gynecological or fetal interference, are more common in the abductees who work with Hopkins. There are details of "cell-sampling," leaving "long, thin scalpel-like incisions" and "round, deep scoop marks" in the skin. There is a tale of an abductee dropped from a height of five feet onto her bedroom floor. We read of alienation and fear, of repeated

abductions, of all sorts of trauma and difficulty; and some of this is emerging without the need for hypnosis.

Here we see abductees thinking in terms of "fighting back" against their persecutors, of refusing to "interbreed" with "questionable creatures." However these images and memories come into the consciousness of individuals, it is not surprising that those who feel they have experienced abduction by aliens should want to seek help and support.

> ## Dream and fantasy, illusion and hallucination may seem real to those in whose mind they are perceived.

Given the intensity of all this belief, and the responses to it, can we continue to insist that abductions are not real events? It is no help at all to say, as many commentators have, that "they are real to those who experience them." Dream and fantasy, illusion and hallucination may seem real to those in whose mind they are perceived. But subjective perception is poor evidence

Ghosts and aliens
Perhaps the closest parallel to an extraterrestrial sighting is the vision of a ghost. In both experiences the witness is usually alone, and in a state of fear. In both cases public opinion is divided as to whether the phenomenon is real or a figment of the witness's imagination. This illustration of a ghostly visitation accompanied William Makepeace Thackeray's poem "The Cane-bottom'd Chair" in an 1894 edition of The Graphic *magazine.*

indeed for objective reality — whether an event actually occurred. Investigators of all kinds of extraordinary events always benefit from considering the historical background of any type of experience. With abductions, we are not only looking at a type that scarcely occurred before the 1960's, but which has developed in complexity and sophistication in the relatively few years since, until there is little variation in reports from a wide range of sources.

A recent obsession

A number of questions therefore present themselves. If people from other planets really are coming to visit us, why have they done so only recently? Why have they suddenly become obsessed with sexual and genetic issues? If we take a few steps back into the history of the

---

How come in the 1950's the aliens were so different, being jolly spacemen with kooky names?

---

subject, how come in the 1950's the aliens were so different, being jolly spacemen with kooky names, and a desire to protect the human race from nuclear warfare or natural disaster? And why didn't the contactees then need hypnosis to remember what had happened to them?

History is full of visionaries, mystics, mediums, and magicians. There are innumerable accounts of apparently normal and intelligent people who have reported encounters with nonhuman beings. These include demons, fairies, and ghosts, as well as a wide variety of traditional religious figures. As a race, we have been dealing with aliens as far back as history is recorded, and probably further. Perhaps it is the way we see these aliens that changes, rather than the aliens themselves? Does the core of the actual experience — be it "real" or "psychological" — remain intrinsically the same, being interpreted differently depending on the perceiver and the society around him or her? The abduction phenomenon looks like an

Dr. Jean Mundy

Dr. Rima E. Laibow

extreme form of this type of experience: a form suitable for the latter part of a confused century, one in which many established patterns of religious and other faith have broken down.

Although there have been religious movements in the past based on similar experiences, there have been few where so many people claim actually to have made contact with the alien beings.

Traditionally, religions are divided into priests and people: but the abduction movement has the advantage that anyone can join the priesthood. To take the parallel one step further, the hypnosis-counseling-therapy element of the investigation can be seen as a form of initiation process, as the seeker becomes one of the chosen.

Unwilling victims?

We cannot, of course, prove that abductions are not real. And any claim of extraordinary experience, if made sincerely, should be treated with the utmost respect. But if we can genuinely fit the phenomena, and the reactions to it, into such clear historical contexts as those of nonhuman contact, and of traditional forms of religious behavior, then it seems reasonable to suppose that these are not new phenomena, unique to our time. This leaves a tremendous mystery to be unraveled, but it may not be the mystery that we started with. We may not be the unwilling victims that the abductees fear we are.

WHO ARE THE ABDUCTEES?

When *Omni* magazine asked its readers "Have you been abducted?" they received about 2,000 letters. Dr. Jean Mundy, an experienced psychologist, studied the responses and concluded that, in general, the writers were "without psychiatric disorder."

Investigations conducted by Dr. Michael A. Persinger, a clinical neuropsychologist, show such people as likely to be sensitive, creative, intuitive, and artistic. But many abductees have been "victims" from their early years onwards.

A New York psychiatrist, Dr. Rima E. Laibow, reports that over half the abductees she has studied have also been physically or sexually abused as children. A conventional explanation therefore presents itself: the abduction story has been invented by the subject's subconscious as a screen for the even more painful memories of abuse by a trusted adult.

Deep in the mind

But Dr. Laibow's findings do not support this. Why, she points out, is the abduction experience in most cases so deep in the mind that it can only be fully revealed by hypnosis? If it were a screen, it should be in the conscious mind, which is where the abuse experience is found. And in none of the cases she studied was there any confusion of scars caused by the physical abuse and those attributed to the abduction.

It is impossible to identify an abductee "type." However, a psychological background of trauma, hardship, and abuse is common to many psychics and mediums. Difficult childhood experiences may heighten sensitivity and render a person more susceptible to extreme experience later in life.

THE BELIEVERS

Throughout the world an increasing number of people believe that beings from other planets can offer them a way to personal salvation.

"*R*IGHT NOW, ALL OVER THE WORLD, certain men and women are responding to some remarkable internal stimulus....They are having peculiar memories surface which remind them that their true ancestral home is a very distant, a very alien 'somewhere else.'"

So begins *The Star People* (1981) by Brad and Francie Steiger, with its startling hypothesis that there are thousands of aliens now awakening among us. According to Brad Steiger, a prolific author of books on UFO's, these are the Star People, whose ancestors were alien beings who visited our earth, and interbred with humans. He claims that genetic traces may still be found in these individuals today in the form of extra vertebrae, unusual blood types, low body temperature, or chronic sinusitis.

Star People

Steiger says that he first became aware of this group of people when he traveled across the U.S.A. on lecture tours, gathering material for his books and articles. Individuals would make themselves known to him and tell him their memories of their alien ancestry. Soon Steiger had encountered enough people across the country who had the same memories to prompt him to investigate this phenomenon.

He believes that the Star People are men and women who have an awareness that their "soul essence" came to earth from other worlds. These reawakened people are now waiting to help us through "the very difficult times which lie ahead...terrible cataclysms, volcanisms, geological changes, the collapse of social structures...maybe even the reversal of the planet's electromagnetic field or the shifting of its magnetic poles." Steiger found that the majority of the Star People are already working for the benefit of the community, as doctors, teachers, police officers, or even psychic counselors.

Starbirth Questionnaire

Steiger subsequently devised the Starbirth Questionnaire, which claims to help you assess your own Star Person potential. The test includes 33 questions, such as: "Did you feel your mother and father were not your true parents?"; "Did you have unseen friends as a child?"; "Do you have mesmerizing eyes?"; and "Please state the event that occurred to you around the age of five. Tell who or what you saw. Please state what message, if any, was given."

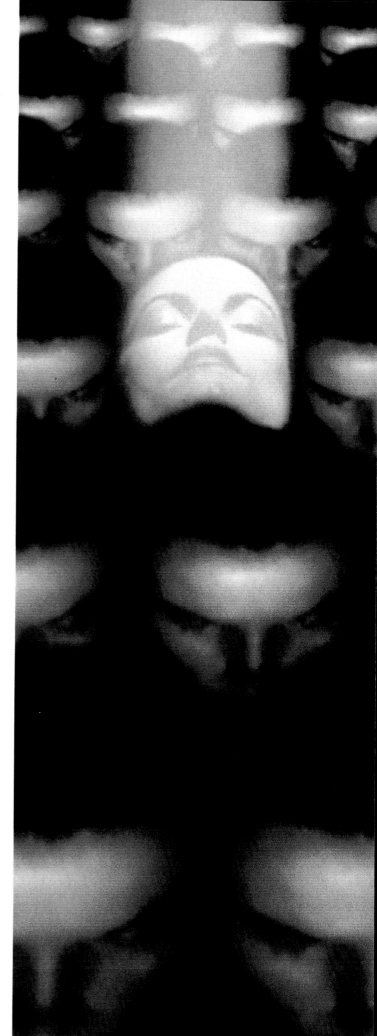

Harvest of believers
Researchers who investigate cults formed around alien intelligences have identified the elements that are needed to hold a group of believers together. These include receiving messages from the aliens, a charismatic leader, an explanation of a UFO mystery, and some joint task for members to work at, such as preparing for the aliens' arrival on the planet.

Starman
This 1984 movie starred Nancy Allen and Jeff Bridges.

The Man Who Fell to Earth
David Bowie took the title role in this 1976 movie.

STAR ALIENS

Both these modern science fiction movies recreate situations that might well have occurred if alien beings had really visited our planet. In *Starman* the alien comes to earth in human guise, and wins the trust of those with whom he comes in contact. Before he returns to his home planet, he fathers a Starseed child.

However, in *The Man Who Fell to Earth* the alien visitor distrusts everybody he meets and so in turn meets with this response from all who come into contact with him. He is eventually destroyed.

Other questions relate to health, personal habits, and appearance. All are leading questions that look for indications in the individual that will mark him or her as different. The questions are direct. Steiger does not claim to be subtle; he knows precisely what information he is looking for, and he thinks he has isolated a way of finding it.

Over 20,000 people have answered the Starbirth Questionnaire. Steiger's analysis of the incoming questionnaires breaks down as follows. He considers 36 percent of the respondents to be Starseed — that is, earthlings whose genes carry inherent characteristics of their extraterrestrial ancestors. A further 47 percent proved to be Star Helpers, the descendants of the first disciples of the aliens when they visited our planet. The remaining 17 percent who answered the questionnaire were found to be men and women who are all obviously fascinated by the work and are themselves quite probably evolving toward increased spiritual awareness. Other details that emerged are that 92 percent felt their mother and father were not their true parents; 80 percent had unseen friends and had been visited by an "angel, elf, or Light Being" at around the age of five. Many were inexplicably drawn to the constellation Sirius, and 7 percent had heard the

message that "Now is the time." According to the guidelines set out by Steiger, over a third of those who completed the questionnaire believed their ancestry to be extraterrestrial. This is astonishing enough in itself, but what is perhaps even more striking is the unmistakable parallels between the

---

Over a third of those who completed the Starbirth Questionnaire believed their ancestry to be extraterrestrial.

---

abductee stories and the experience of the Star People. In both cases, people are often contacted by alien beings while very young. These individuals may have always felt that they were outsiders, alien, and separate, not truly belonging to this world. In both experiences the individuals are then activated in some way later in life, in some cases claiming to have found their true purpose.

The Starseed experience

In Steiger's early publications he saw the abductee experience as something dangerous and unpleasant. But the *Gods of Aquarius* (published in 1976) and *The Star People* (1981) are optimistic about humankind's contact with the aliens. Time and again, the overriding emotion abductees experience is that of powerlessness. The Starseed experience is much closer to the thinking of the New Age movement, in which people believe that they can control their destiny through positive thinking, and so live their lives with greater spiritual awareness. Channeling is a modern form of mediumship in which

Ashtar Space Command logo

spirit guides speak through a human being — the channeler. In the more traditional form of spiritualist mediumship, spirits strive to connect with our world by establishing that they are, for example, the spirit of a dead person. The "channeling" movement is based on the idea that alien intelligences from other worlds, or even dimensions, are communicating with us. Channelers do not attempt to prove the truth of the messages they receive; they simply wish to pass them on.

Ashtar Space Command
There is a tremendous variety of communicators and messages, and channeling has achieved remarkable popularity in recent years in the U.S.A. Cults have developed around individual channelers. Ashtar Space Command, based in Salt Lake City, Utah, is one such. Here the interplanetary space commander Ashtar communicates through Tuella, a gentle, rather unassuming woman from Durango, Colorado. Tuella gives messages concerning an impending planetary catastrophe. This apocalypse will be

followed by what she calls "harvest," when spiritually developed people will survive on earth with the aid of the friendly aliens.

Aetherius Society
Contacts of this kind are not just a recent development. The Aetherius Society has headquarters in London and Los Angeles, and has flourished for more than 30 years, in a field where belief groups are not longlasting.

The Aetherius Society has developed a detailed cosmology which it claims explains why so many flying saucers are witnessed on earth. They are the emissaries of the benign and concerned Interplanetary Parliament. The Aetherius Society was founded by George King, who claimed to be the earthly ambassador of this parliament.

Aetherius Society members are encouraged to work with the extraterrestrials who come into earth's

▶ PAGE 112

Space talk
Tuella communicates to her followers at the Guardian International Annual Congress the messages the space commander Ashtar has channeled through her. A common theme found throughout Tuella's pronouncements is that now it is time for the "eartheans" to put aside their old ways and become part of the New World Order.

WHEN PROPHECY FAILS
In *When Prophecy Fails* (1956) coauthors Leon Festinger, Henry Riecken, and Stanley Schachter, all of them sociologists, give a detailed account of the rise and fall of a UFO belief group.

"Marian Keech" of "Lake City," Utah (her true name and the location are not revealed), claimed she was communicating with aliens on the planet Clarion. A cult called the Seekers formed around Keech, and she soon began to receive specific messages.

The flood
One in particular caught the public's imagination. This told how at dawn on December 21, 1954, "Lake City" would be destroyed by a flood that would create an inland sea from the Arctic Circle to the Gulf of Mexico. Keech told her followers that provided they prepared correctly they would not be drowned but would be carried away in flying saucers.

In the last days before December 21, Keech received increasingly outlandish messages. Cult members gave up jobs, possessions, and partners. The need for all metal

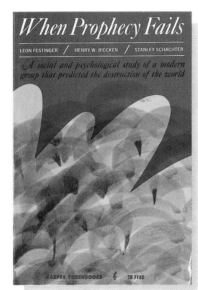

to be removed from clothes and bodies prior to the escape caused some lively discussions about zippers, brassieres, and dental fillings. However, their hopes were raised only to be dashed; the flood did not occur as prophesied.

Collapse of the cult
On December 24, 1954, a crowd of more than 200 believers surrounded Keech's house, chanting for the aliens to come. They would not be moved, and eventually the police had to be called. Within days the "Lake City" community began to make life difficult for the Seekers, accusing them of exerting undue influence on their children. Keech and other cult members had to go into hiding, and after a brief period of stubborn resistance, the cult broke up.

The Seekers may sound like the stuff of fiction, and indeed, Alison Lurie's book *Imaginary Friends* (1967) tells a similar story. In this book a New England cult called the Truth Seekers live according to the messages channeled from a spirit guide named Ro through a beautiful young woman called Verena.

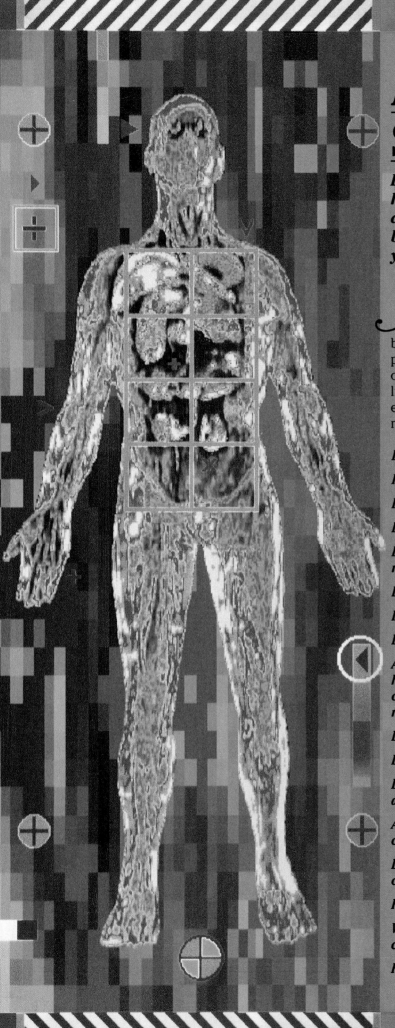

ARE YOU A STAR PERSON?

Brad Steiger, author of The Star People, has devised a questionnaire to help people discover if they are descended from alien beings who visited earth thousands of years ago, or from their original disciples.

ACCORDING TO STEIGER, Star People share many experiences — a feeling that they do not really belong on earth, visitations from otherworldly beings when they were children, as well as certain physical anomalies. Steiger believes that Star People are often the result of unplanned pregnancies, thrive on little sleep, and appear hypersensitive to electricity and electromagnetic force fields. If you can answer yes to most of these questions, you too may be a Star Person.

Do you have an unusual blood type?

Is your body temperature low?

Do you have low blood pressure?

Do you have extra vertebrae?

Do you suffer from painful joints, headaches, or severe neck pain?

Do you suffer from chronic sinusitis?

Do you long to return to your true home?

Did you have imaginary playmates as a child?

Are you strongly attracted to willow trees, hummingbirds, eagles, rocks, stars, lilacs, natural crystals, mushrooms, darkness, electrical storms, nature, or the name Leah?

Do you have mesmerizing eyes?

Do you see bright lights when your eyes are closed?

Do you often hear a strange noise, a whine, a click, or a buzzing sound, before a psychic experience?

Are you attracted to the planet Venus or the constellation Sirius?

Did you have a psychic experience when you were a child, at age five or six?

Have you ever had a message saying "Now is the time"?

When you were about 11, did anything happen to change your lifestyle or your attitudes?

Have you ever been visited by otherworldly entities?

Are You an Abductee?

Do you have recurring nightmares? Do you experience temporary paralysis on awakening? Is there a period of time for which you cannot account? If so, you may have had an alien abduction experience.

*E*VERYONE HAS A PERFECT subconscious memory of everything that has ever happened to him or her, claims psychologist Edith Fiore in her book *Abductions* (1989). She found that many of her patients had been traumatized by close encounters with extraterrestrials that remained hidden deep in their subconscious. According to Fiore, if you can answer yes to most questions on this checklist, then you too may have been abducted by aliens.

Have you experienced a period of time for which you cannot account?

Do you suffer from any sleep disorders?

Do you have nightmares or dreams of aliens or UFO's?

Do you have the same recurring dream?

Do you have flashbacks of your dreams?

On waking, do you have unusual bodily sensations such as tingling, numbness, or temporary paralysis?

Have any unexplained marks appeared on your body?

Are there any bruises that look as if blood has been drawn from your body?

Have you found any new fine red lines or scars on your body?

Do you suffer from nosebleeds or bleeding from your ears or find spots of blood on your sheets that cannot be explained?

Do you feel as if you are being monitored, watched over, and/or being contacted by UFO's or aliens?

Do you have repeated UFO sightings?

Do you have a vague memory of a close encounter with an alien?

Are you aware of some unexplained healing? Have you found yourself spontaneously cured of some illness?

Do you experience an irrational fear or anxiety, or any bodily sensation when UFO's or extraterrestrials are mentioned?

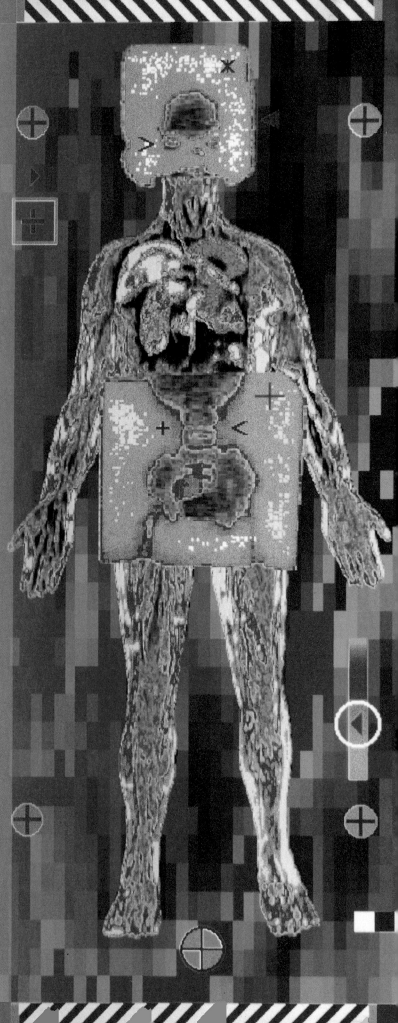

The Unarius Star Center
The Unarius Academy of Science is based in California. It holds an annual congress at which Uriel receives messages of peace and love from representatives of all 33 planets in the confederation. This room at the academy is a futuristic view of another world.

orbit. Together they claim to invoke and store spiritual energy in "prayer batteries" through prayer and the chanting of sacred mantras. This energy can then be discharged as necessary, to prevent hardship, disease, and disaster around the world. In the course of this work, society members have made pilgrimages to charge spiritual batteries in such harsh and mountainous terrain as Ben Macdhui in Scotland, Mount Kilimanjaro in Tanzania, and the Madrigerfluh in Switzerland. While this cult may seem farfetched, it is difficult to doubt the commitment of its members.

Few cults or belief groups last long without there being some specific purpose for their members to work toward. This may be as simple as spreading the message that there are Space Brothers out there. It may be as technical as building a flying saucer. Or it may even be as ambitious as saving the earth from imminent destruction. All these tasks demand considerable faith on the part of group members, and a real sense of relationship with and deep commitment to their own particular group of aliens. Such groups of believers first began to appear in the

Ruth E. Norman, channeler for Uriel

1950's, with the emergence of the first contactees. There are still those who believe that intelligent life exists on nearby planets even though space exploration has disproved this beyond any reasonable doubt. One such group, the Star Fellowship, based in Surrey, England, follows the beliefs of one of the first contactees, George Adamski. In a booklet entitled *The Inhabited Solar System*, the Star Fellowship argues that there is life on other planets in our solar system. They also provide a glossary of a language called Solexmal, which they claim to be "the apparent interlingua of the Solar System."

Uriel

Perhaps the most comprehensive belief system is that of the Unarius Academy of Science, based in El Cajon, California. Headed by Ruth E. Norman, a channeler for Uriel (Universal Radiant Infinite Eternal Light), its philosophy combines many strands of New Age thinking, including spiritual development and reincarnation, and places a special

The followers of Uriel assert that spacecraft "buzz" the earth bringing healing radiations of love.

emphasis on UFO's and their occupants. The word Unarius is itself an acronym for Universal Articulate Interdimensional Understanding of Science.

The Unarius cosmology has earth (otherwise known as Ioshanna) as one of the 33 planets of the Interplanetary Confederation. (Details of the populations and characteristics are given, but this does not include pinpointing the whereabouts of these planets.) It predicts a tremendous landing on earth in the year 2001 by spacecraft from the rest of the confederation, ushering in a millennium of contentment and culture on this previously troubled earth.

Uriel also brings messages from great thinkers such as Albert Einstein, who are now working with the aliens. Napoleon also communicates with Uriel, as does

Operation prayer power
Aetherius Society members believe that prayer can be stored in special batteries, for later use where it is most needed. Here a group use the psychic point in their palms to channel energy into the battery.

the ancient Greek historian Herodotus. One of the Unarius Academy of Science's most intriguing publications is their booklet *Facts about UFO's*. This attempts to explain the reported behavior of UFO's. It has become important for such an organization to give UFO's a good press because in recent years alien spacecraft and their occupants have been interpreted as destructive and evil.

Demon UFO's
There is even a line of Fundamentalist thought that argues that UFO's are piloted by demons, seducing humankind into thinking that these entities are more powerful than God. *Flying Saucer Review* regularly discusses the possibility that UFO entities have long been interpreted as *djinns*, the supernatural creatures of Islamic theology who can take on human form and work on behalf of evil forces.

Emphasizing the positive and constructive aspects, the followers of Uriel assert that spacecraft "buzz" the earth, bringing "healing radiations of love and light" to eliminate public fears before each landing. The occupants are "beautiful, tall beings of love," who first came to earth 165,000 years ago. According to members of the Unarius Academy, the aliens do not look like E.T.; the four-foot tall dwarves repeatedly reported by abductees are nothing but robots. Abduction by aliens, they claim, is a wonderful experience. Sometimes

the abductee changes in atomic structure to "a fourth-dimensional energy being."

Members of the Unarius cult are not the only ones who explain alien contact in this way. Another fascinating group, called the Light Affiliates, is based in Burnaby, British Columbia, Canada. They were informed by an extraterrestrial called Ox-Ho that the Day of Judgment would be on November 22, 1969.

The chosen few
Fortunately for cult members, the Space Brothers had their interests at heart. They were going to "remove the Chosen and return them to earth after the planet had once again 'crystallized.'" Even more practical measures were in hand at the Michigan Institute for Cosmic Research. Here, a young man known as Gordon claimed that he was instructed by the Intergalactic Council to build a flying saucer called the *Bluebird*.

There are a number of cults worldwide based on a belief in alien beings, and new ones are being formed all the time. These groups have no interest in having their beliefs subjected to the strictures of scientific testing. Faith and enthusiasm are the twin keys to membership.

Shirley MacLaine
In her book Dancing in the Light (1985) *New Ager MacLaine describes the transformation in her life brought about by her quest for spiritual growth.*

NEW AGERS
The New Age movement represents a shift away from the materialism of the late 20th century. It encourages individuals to develop a greater awareness of their human spirit and potential, the world they live in, and the universe of which they are part.

Channeling
This is a technique common to spiritualist mediumship, believers in extraterrestrial life, and New Agers. In all cases, the voices of the spirit guides speaking from other worlds and dimensions have a common purpose in educating humankind and passing on information of various kinds.

Most people who believe they have had contact with alien life-forms claim a transformation in their lives. In most cases, this is a positive experience. This is similar to the effect experienced by New Agers when they get in touch with their higher selves.

Government cover-up?
Some ufologists claim that there is a conspiracy to hush up UFO reports. Stories such as these in sci-fi comics and the popular press help to keep the debate alive.

CONSPIRACY OR DELUSION?

Since the earliest UFO sightings, the U.S. Air Force and the CIA have been accused of interfering with serious attempts to investigate and evaluate them.

FROM THE U.S. AIR FORCE's first study of UFO's, Project Sign in 1948, to the Condon Report published two decades later, government projects set up ostensibly for the scientific study of UFO's quickly became debunking exercises. The CIA's Robertson panel, reporting in 1953, gave an insight into the position of all such government investigations by recommending that "the national security agencies take immediate steps to strip the Unidentified Flying Objects of the special status they have been given and the aura of mystery they have unfortunately acquired."

Official stories

The summaries of the various government reports released to the press and publicized often told a very different story from their detailed contents. Of the 87 sightings studied in the Condon Report, 25 percent remained unexplained, yet its summary stated that "Careful consideration of the record...leads us to conclude that further extensive study of UFO's probably cannot be justified...." Why was the committee so eager to deny the evidence of its own report and insist that UFO's do not exist?

There are several hypotheses. One, based on some evidence and much hearsay, holds that alien flying discs have crashed on American soil more than once, and that live aliens have been rescued from the wreckage. If this has happened, the authorities may have reasons to keep it secret.

Differing theories

It has been claimed that the aliens have assisted in U.S. and other space projects, by passing on their own advanced scientific information. In exchange for this help, they have been allowed to continue unmolested in their study — some say guidance — of our planet and its peoples.

There are two flaws in this theory. If alien spacecraft can maneuver and accelerate in the astonishing fashion reported by those who have seen them in action, why cannot ours, after more than four decades of alleged contact and technological exchange? The second flaw lies in the continued secrecy of such a conspiracy. Surely someone would have exposed it by now, believing that it was in

V-2 rocket
By the end of the Second World War, Germany was the world leader in rocket technology. The U.S.A. experimented with the remaining V-2 rockets for several years after the war while establishing its own rocket program. The flying saucer phenomenon may have been a useful cover for such secret weapons testing.

Sputnik II
A cutaway scale model of the Russians' space probe was put on show at the World's Fair in Brussels, Belgium, in 1958. The UFO phenomenon may have helped to divert attention away from the Soviets' definite lead over the U.S.A. in the space race.

the public interest that people should know what was going on? However, even if the UFO's are not alien spacecraft, governments may have good reasons to manipulate the widespread belief that they are. Perhaps they are, in fact, secret weapons or aircraft. The government and military keep these craft secret by encouraging interest in UFO's, for even if such clandestine weapons systems stray into public view, they will be interpreted as "flying saucers." Witnesses can then be dismissed as cranks, and the objects themselves can be explained away as civilian aircraft or natural phenomena.

William H. Spaulding, a director of the Arizona-based organization Ground Saucer Watch (GSW), first developed this argument, which he called the "federal hypothesis," after a careful analysis of hundreds of top-secret UFO-related documents declassified under the Freedom of Information Act.

Secret weapons tests
Spaulding noted that areas of high UFO activity in the U.S.A. were near test sites for secret weapons and aircraft. The notorious flying saucer crash reported near Roswell, New Mexico, in July 1947 was within a few days of the launch of a

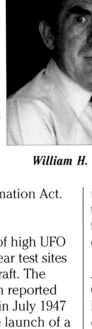

William H. Spaulding

Areas of high UFO activity in the U.S.A. were near test sites for secret weapons and aircraft.

V-2 rocket by the nearby White Sands Missile Range. At about the same time, the U.S. Army sent up one of its first polyethylene weather research balloons. Either of these, going off course, could have been responsible for the wreckage. The witnesses' reports of an "incredibly tough" material unlike anything they had ever seen could refer to polyethylene — uncommon in the late 1940's.

Distracted by UFO's
Spaulding suspected that several aspects of the UFO phenomenon might be attributable to interference run by the CIA or some group within it. He noted that waves of American UFO sightings frequently followed moments of crisis for the U.S. government. A cluster of sightings in New Mexico and Texas followed the Soviets' successful launch of Sputnik II (only 30 days after Sputnik I) in November 1957. On December 6, 1957, the U.S. space program suffered an ignominious, televised failure of Vanguard TV-3, and the UFO scare was a very welcome distraction.

A UFO conspiracy backed up by the military would protect secret weapons from prying eyes. Disinformation would divert the scientific community from a serious study of the UFO phenomenon. A few bogus cases, set up years apart, would be enough to fuel the mystery and keep ufologists and the media busy. Behind this useful smokescreen, secret technology and unusual aircraft designs could be tested.

An invisible aircraft
One specific, recorded instance will illustrate how this campaign of disinformation works. Since 1966 the U.S. Air Force has been developing Stealth technology (electronic evasion equipment such as that used in the B-2 bomber). In 1975 an air force mobile radar unit picked up an aircraft leaving Edwards Air Force Base, California, at over 460 m.p.h. In one sweep of the radar, the blip had vanished — a feat possible, in theory, only if the target had accelerated to over 2,000 m.p.h. This was reported as another case of a UFO spying on a military installation. In fact, this turned out to be a plane testing Stealth technology. By simply switching on its electronic countermeasures systems in that sweep of the radar, it had become electronically invisible. It also became invisible in another sense: behind the story that it was a UFO.

THE MJ-12 AFFAIR

In 1987 the disclosure of top-secret documents caused a sensation. They appeared to prove that the U.S. government had conspired to cover up a flying saucer crash. They were later revealed as forgeries, but this left a further mystery to solve.

WHEN LOS ANGELES TV PRODUCER Jaime Shandera opened the unsolicited package placed in his mailbox on December 11, 1984, he found photocopies of two documents, one dated September 24, 1947, the other November 18, 1952. The first was signed by President Harry S. Truman. The second was addressed to President Dwight D. Eisenhower by Adm. Roscoe H. Hillenkoetter, a former director of the CIA. Both were marked TOP SECRET.

Jaime Shandera

A board of experts

The document signed by Truman purported to be a classified executive order to Secretary of Defense James V. Forrestal. It authorized him, after due consultation with nuclear scientist Dr. Vannevar Bush, to establish a board of experts to be answerable directly and only to the president, and to be known as Majestic 12 (or simply MJ-12). Their job was to investigate the case of the flying saucer that had crashed near Roswell, New Mexico, in July 1947.

Here, it seemed, was proof that the crashed flying saucer, long a subject of rumor and speculation among ufologists, had really happened. The second document backed up the first. It was a top-secret briefing for the newly elected president on the members and progress of the MJ-12 group.

Crashed-saucer experts

In view of the extraordinary nature of the MJ-12 documents, it seems strange that Shandera waited over two years before making them public, on May 29, 1987. Shandera's associates in the revelation were the writers William L. Moore, who coauthored *The Roswell Incident* with Charles Berlitz (author of *The Bermuda Triangle*), and crashed-saucer expert Stanton T.

Harry S. Truman

Freedman. The theories of both Moore and Freedman stood to be vindicated if the papers were real. Shandera, however, claims that he does not know who sent him the material nor why he was chosen to receive it.

Shandera, Moore, and Freedman then claimed to have found further documentary backing for the existence of MJ-12. They said that they were in contact with a "highly placed military intelligence operative" who could authenticate the story outlined in the letters. Their source was discredited, however, when he turned out to be a lowly U.S. Air Force sergeant once found guilty of falsifying documents.

The papers themselves soon took a battering. Analysts found that the machine used to type the Truman "executive order" of 1947 was a Smith-Corona model that had not been manufactured until 1963. Hillenkoetter's memorandum to Eisenhower was dated in an odd mixture of civilian and military styles. Furthermore, Hillenkoetter had apparently signed himself "Roscoe H. Hillenkoetter" — which is not a form that appears before or since in any of his voluminous surviving correspondence. Finally, a close inspection of the signature on the Truman document showed that it was a photocopy of the signature on a letter from Truman to Dr. Bush, written on October 1, 1947. As the Hillenkoetter memo of 1952 refers specifically to the Truman "special classified executive order" of 1947, it follows that both are fakes.

Careless forgeries

This is an unusual case of a conspiracy to invent a conspiracy. But who was scheming against whom is not immediately clear. The clumsiness of the hoax suggests that it may have been intended to be exposed. In that case it may have been the work of the CIA, in an attempt to discredit the pro-UFO groups. But it seems likely that a pro-UFO group simply invented the evidence that they were convinced really existed. Anyone who stumbles across faked evidence that at first sight appears to prove their theory will, with good reason, be the first to come under suspicion.

James V. Forrestal

THE MEN IN BLACK

Men in Black are mysterious figures in dark suits who are said to menace UFO witnesses. But who they are and where they come from is not known.

AN ENCOUNTER WITH Men in Black (MIB) is said to be among the most disturbing experiences a UFO witness can have. Reported MIB encounters seem to follow a pattern: the witness, usually male, decides to report the UFO sighting. Immediately after he reports it, and even in some cases before, two men dressed in conservative dark suits, often with white shirts, black ties, and dark hats, call at the witness's home. They look like FBI agents from a Hollywood B-movie, although they usually seem suntanned and have an oriental slant to their eyes. They may flash badges or other forms of ID and claim to be from some obscure-sounding government department.

MIB are often said to look awkward and ill-at-ease, generally talking in the melodramatic but slightly stilted slang of a 1940's Hollywood scriptwriter. In 1967 Robert Richardson sent an investigatory group a piece of metal he found after an encounter with a UFO. MIB went to his home, he said, and told him to get it back, with the warning: "...if you want your wife to stay as pretty as she is." MIB are often reported to threaten that a UFO witness or his family will suffer if he breathes a word of his sighting to anybody.

Aliens acting human

The cars MIB drive seem odd, too. Generally they are reported to be brand-new vehicles, although the model in question may have been out of production for 20 years or more. They are always prestige models: usually Cadillacs in North America, Jaguars in the UK and Europe. The license plates, when checked out, are unissued numbers. Frequently a third MIB is said to stay in the car during the interview, sometimes sitting in a purplish glow.

The most rational explanation of MIB is that they are hallucinations of some kind, although why they are so consistent in their appearance (and they have visited people all over the world who know little or nothing of UFO lore) remains a real enigma. The extreme interpretation is that they are aliens masquerading as human beings, basing their performances on government agents as portrayed in popular culture.

A more complex theory is that they may be part of some elaborate psychological experiment, or a deliberate test of UFO witnesses' integrity. But however alarming MIB are at the time, their threats are always empty, and they are ultimately harmless.

CHAPTER FIVE

UNRAVELING THE ENIGMA

For over 50 years there have been reports periodically of strange, unidentified craft flying over our planet. How much progress have we made in our attempts to make sense of this phenomenon?

In July 1947 an American had only to open a newspaper to be inundated with UFO reports. In that one month, researcher Ted Bloecher noted the following cases: At Twin Falls, Idaho, 60 picnickers watched three formations of more than 35 objects flying overhead; at Hauser Lake, near Spokane, more than 200 people saw a lone disc in the sky; the entire crew of a United Air Lines flight watched two groups of discs near the Idaho-Oregon

The original "flying saucers"
The UFO craze can be dated back to June 24, 1947, when pilot Kenneth Arnold saw a formation of disc-shaped objects over the Cascade Range in Washington State. This illustration is an artist's reconstruction of that extraordinary event.

Earthquake lights
This photograph was taken during a series of earthquakes at Matsushiro in Japan between 1965 and 1967. The photograph is regarded as scientific evidence that strain on the earth's crust can produce light phenomena. The Canadian researcher Dr. Michael Persinger has made a strong case that natural light phenomena are at the bottom of many UFO sightings, and this is supported by Paul Devereux, author of Earth Lights Revelation *(1989)*.

border at dusk; dozens of police and scores of citizens reported a large number of discs flying over Portland, Oregon; in Seattle, a coastguardsman took the first widely published photograph of a flying disc.

From the day in June 1947 that pilot Kenneth Arnold reported his flying saucer sighting, there were those who believed that flying saucers were really physical objects. The fact that the publication of his story was at once followed by other claims suggested to some observers that the American public had been caught up in a collective fantasy.

Mass hysteria
In the view of Gordon Atwater, curator of the Hayden Museum and Planetarium in New York, the flying saucer phenomenon was a mild case of meteorological jitters, with mass hysteria thrown in. Psychologist Leo Crespi, of the Office of Public Opinion Research, thought that the saucers were the projection of a delusion.

But how could such views prevail against the fact that more and more sincere and intelligent witnesses were claiming to have seen structured objects, with clearly defined shapes, flashing lights, and other physical details? How could all these sightings be dismissed as natural phenomena, wrongly identified? It seemed even less reasonable to write them off as hallucinations. Had these witnesses, in effect, seen nothing at all?

Even today we find it hard to believe that so many witnesses could be mistaken: nonetheless, this view is being seriously entertained. Two important factors have contributed to bring this about. First, there is the dismaying fact that although the UFO's are supposed to have been intruding into our airspace for close to half a century, they have left behind them not a scrap of truly conclusive physical evidence to back up what the many eyewitnesses claim to have seen.

Second, investigators have come to the painful realization that no matter how sincere a witness may be, however clear in his or her mind, he or she may nevertheless be mistaken. Though telling the truth, it is only the truth as he or she sees it; and this can be quite different from what someone else might see in the same place at the same time.

No matter how sincere a witness may be, he or she may nevertheless be mistaken.

In November 1977 four unsuspecting people stepped off a bus in the suburbs of Manchester, England, and became aware of some strange lights in the sky. All four witnesses agreed that they had seen an immense, silent object that one of them described to the police as "like a huge floating restaurant."

How could four people — not known to one another — all agree and yet be mistaken? But equally, how could such an object pass over a vast city like Manchester without being seen by anyone else in the air or on the ground? For those four people to see it, the object surely had to be real. But if real, how could it possibly escape detection by any other witnesses?

Nuts-and-bolts spacecraft
Even accepting that the UFO's could be nuts-and-bolts alien spacecraft does not explain the profusion of paradoxes and ambiguities in the case files. More and more, modern investigators are looking — albeit often with reluctance

and misgivings — at solutions on the very fringe of conventional science.

These fall into two categories. On the one hand are the psychosocial solutions, what have been termed the "all-in-the-mind" approaches. These are based on how individuals can behave in stressful circumstances, and how that behavior may be shaped by social and cultural forces, such as concern about security or the environment.

Contrasting approaches

For example, the sudden wave of UFO sightings in Belgium in the winter of 1989-90 occurred just at the time when the question of reuniting West and East Germany was being debated. The sightings occurred near Belgium's border with Germany. A French ufologist and author, Thierry Pinvidic, has speculated that it is the fear of a reunited Germany — which invaded Belgium in the two World Wars — that lies behind the alleged sightings.

Apparently contrasting with such "all-in-the-mind" approaches are those that propose forces hitherto unrecognized by science. These may be geo-physical or meteorological, producing phenomena ranging from earthquake lights to ball lightning, from will-o'-the-wisp to spook lights. The existence of all of these is very well established, but little is known about their true nature.

Other theories are more bizarre, involving unrecognized life-forms sharing our atmosphere. This would account for the many reports of the UFO's behaving in an apparently intelligent manner.

However, it is hard to believe that any such forces or life-forms could have succeeded in escaping the attention of science. Other researchers are proposing that the human mind may be interacting with an unknown phenomenon. Could both approaches — the "all-in-the-mind" and the "unknown-natural-cause" way — actually come together?

Germany reunited
There were jubilant scenes as the wall between East and West Berlin was dismantled in the fall of 1989. This photograph was taken on November 11, Veterans Day, when by tradition the war dead are remembered. It has been suggested that subconscious fears of a strong, united Germany may be responsible for some UFO sightings of that period.

FLIGHTS OF FANCY

Serious debate about the nature of UFO's is undermined by wild claims made by fringe ufologists. Here is a sample of the more outrageous rumors that have found their way into print:

Shipwrecked aliens

It is claimed that in 1947 a flying saucer crashed on American soil. The U.S. government moved quickly to conceal this fact from the public. The bodies of the aliens were housed in an unmarked hangar on a U.S. Air Force base. This momentous secret has been passed, by word of mouth, from president to president ever since.

Scientific advisers

Some visitors may be here to help us. There are rumors that alien doctors are working with the Mexican government in an attempt to find a cure for cancer. Alien technology has also been held responsible for the amazingly advanced design of the U.S. Air Force's new Stealth bombers.

Others believe that there is more to the ancient wonder of the Sphinx than meets the eye. There is a rumor that an authentic spacecraft lies in a secret chamber beneath the monument. It is argued that the ancient Egyptians, with their limited technology, must have had unearthly help to have built such great edifices as the Sphinx and the pyramids.

Diplomatic relations

It has been asserted that the U.S. and Soviet governments were so worried about the threat of an alien invasion that, despite their unfriendly relations during the cold war, they signed a secret mutual aid treaty in case of alien attack. Extremists say that such precautions came too late! Secret UFO bases are said to exist already in Antarctica, off the U.S. coast, and on an uninhabited island off the coast of Wales.

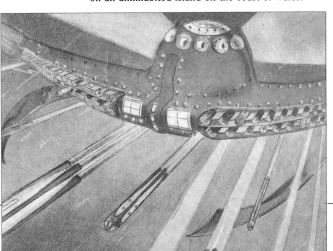

Crashed saucer
A mysterious object that was reported to be a flying saucer crashed in Texas in 1950. It was claimed by radio commentator Henry J. Taylor to be in reality a secret military device.

Hostile aliens
This illustration from an Italian magazine reflects the deep-rooted fears of many people: that we may be invaded by aliens having all the advantages of technological superiority.

UNCONSCIOUS FORCES

Almost 50 percent of U.S. citizens believe in flying saucers, according to a 1987 Gallup poll. Why is the human mind prepared to accept such apparently incredible stories at face value?

W HEN RESEARCHERS FIRST began to examine the flying saucer phenomenon in the 1940's, they took it for granted that what they were investigating was something as materially real as the rockets that scientists were developing at that time.

Investigators saw it as their job to gather data about what kind of object had been seen, how fast it could fly, how long it was, and so on, as if they were conducting scientific research. They soon discovered that many reports were illusions, misidentifications of known objects in the sky. An aircraft seen from an unaccustomed angle when coming in to land can look very odd. Even the moon can look like an alien spacecraft in certain atmospheric conditions.

Most witnesses of UFO's are respectable, ordinary people. They are rarely concerned with making money or becoming famous from publicizing their experience. They make every effort to report as accurately as possible what it is they think that they have seen.

"It is the witness, not the UFO, who — albeit with the best intentions — leads the investigators astray."

However, this is no proof that the witness has reported an experience precisely. An untrained observer could not be expected to give an accurate estimate of the size, distance, and speed of an object in the sky. Investigators have been forced to acknowledge that witnesses may be influenced by subconscious forces of which they are entirely unaware.

A UFO or Venus?

"It is the witness, not the UFO, who — albeit with the best intentions — leads the investigators astray," asserts Michel Monnerie bluntly. This is not an observation by a skeptical outsider. Monnerie is a noted French UFO researcher with years of fine fieldwork to his credit, and his views cannot be ignored. One of his reports shows just how easily a witness may misinterpret natural phenomena.

"At Lot, France, in May 1972, a woman went onto the balcony of her house to close the shutters. As she did so, she had the distinct feeling that she was being

The brightest light
Venus, center, with Jupiter above it to the left and Saturn above it to the right, is the brightest of these planets in the night sky. In 1972 a Frenchwoman and her family, seeing the planet shining brightly, misinterpreted it as a UFO. Researcher Michel Monnerie proved that Venus was in that sector of the sky at that time, and argued that this was what they had seen.

MICHEL MONNERIE

French ufologist Michel Monnerie believes that the study of UFO's should be conducted by psychologists and sociologists rather than by physicists and aviation experts.

Modern gods

From earliest times people have seen unexplained objects in the skies. In most cases these were attributed to the actions of the gods. In the 20th century, it is the scientists who have undertaken the burden of explaining all these mysterious phenomena.

In the last 40 years, sightings of flying saucers and their study have become part of our modern folklore. At the beginning of the flying saucer era we were poised to voyage beyond our world. Monnerie suggests that we see the same phenomena as our ancient forebears saw, but we now interpret them in a modern way, as evidence of unearthly beings.

Personal experiences

Sightings of UFO's form the basis of ufology. Monnerie argues that the study of UFO's can never be strictly scientific when all the research data is based on personal experience that has not been subjected to any rigorous experimental approach. For example, a formation of clouds passing before the moon can suddenly appear to be a giant wheel, turning in the sky. No sooner has this misjudgment been made by the observer than this shape is embellished with windows, turrets, and even occupants. Such an episode forms the basis of many UFO sightings.

Monnerie's first UFO book
Et si les OVNI's n'existaient pas? *(And what if UFO's don't exist?) was published in 1978.*

125

Jacques Vallée
The French astronomer and computer expert Jacques Vallée does not believe in alien visitation. He puts forward the argument that aliens are an expression of a massive self-education process that is at work within humankind.

watched. She looked up and saw a light which at first she took to be an enormous star. But she realized that it was more like a fireball, emitting colors — orange, green, red, and pink. At one moment it seemed to shrink, at the next it seemed to swell. She called her family out onto the balcony and they all saw the same thing.

"The following evening it returned, and the woman saw it descend, then stop, and make an abrupt movement, then stop again. There were similar performances on succeeding evenings. One night it was so bright as to light up the entire balcony."

Monnerie was able to show that the planet Venus was in that sector of the sky at the time, and this was almost certainly what the woman had seen. He suggested that when she observed the planet it took her by surprise, triggering a "waking dream."

To Monnerie it is clear what has happened. The witness sees something, fails to recognize what it is, and so alters it in the mind's eye, adding details and attributes that transform it into something that is immediately identifiable.

Mysteries in the sky
From earliest time people have been seeing and recording unexplained phenomena in the sky. Several centuries separate these UFO sightings — at Taormina in Sicily in 1954 (above), and at Basel in Switzerland in 1566 (right). But it has been argued that the psychological basis for both of them may well be the same.

Some psychologists believe that, for certain people, UFO's fulfill a need. For such people, sightings take on an almost religious connotation, becoming a symbol of salvation. For others, they are a threat, symbolizing danger.

Alien abductions
If seeing a UFO is so meaningful, how much more exhilarating it must be to meet a spacecraft's occupants! At the time that Monnerie and American UFO investigator Allan Hendry voiced their doubts about the credibility of UFO sightings in the 1970's, only a handful of witnesses had claimed to have been actually abducted by aliens. There was no indication that a decade later alien abduction would have developed into such a widespread phenomenon. Today hundreds of people are claiming abduction experiences. Once again, ufologists are confronted with the

"It was more like a fireball, emitting colors — orange, green, red, and pink."

testimony of witnesses, none of which is corroborated by any really convincing material evidence.

Some investigators have been willing to accept the testimony of abduction by aliens at face value. It is indisputable that hundreds of people, who cannot possibly know of each other's experiences, are all telling what is substantially the same story, not simply in general terms but often in very specific detail.

Another fact, cited as supporting evidence, is that many alleged abductees also turn out to have mysterious marks on their bodies. It has been suggested that these are scars from investigative surgery conducted by aliens, or from alien implants, so that the individual can be monitored by his or her extraterrestrial abductors.

It is also a fact that many witnesses are often very frightened, sometimes even to the point of being emotionally disturbed, by their strange experience.

CASEBOOK
STORM POWER

The spacecraft landed and four aliens emerged, said Liberato. They walked toward him bearing bright lights in their hands. They were only about four feet tall, white-skinned, with flat faces.

O NE STORMY NIGHT in 1976, an illiterate Colombian cattle farmer named Liberato Anibal Quintero returned home to his farmhouse and immediately went to lie down on his hammock. He fell asleep at once, which was completely out of character, as his wife Brunilda told investigators later. While he slept, a violent storm broke, but still Liberato did not stir.

Suddenly Liberato awoke with a start. As he recalled later, he felt as if something was about to happen. He dashed from the house and was drawn as if by some inexplicable force toward the cowsheds. He claims he then saw a large, luminous, egg-shaped spacecraft hovering above the outhouses. It lit up the whole area and gave off intense heat.

Alien close encounter
The spacecraft landed and four aliens emerged, said Liberato. They walked toward him bearing bright lights in their hands. They were only about four feet tall, white-skinned, with flat faces and high cheekbones. Their bulbous eyes seemed to have no lids or lashes. Three of them had long hair and looked as if they were female. Liberato was led on board, where the aliens conducted various medical experiments on him. Finally, an intimate encounter took place between Liberato and the three female aliens.

The next morning, Liberato awoke to find himself lying on the grass just as dawn was breaking. There appeared to be definite marks on the ground where he thought he had seen the mysterious vessel. However, there was no other visible evidence that a spaceship had been there.

Weather-sensitive
Could there be some connection between the thunderstorm, Liberato's strange feelings, and the alien visitation? According to Israeli scientist Felix Gad Sulman, one in three people is sufficiently affected by meteorological conditions to be termed "weather-sensitive." Sulman found that his weather-sensitive subjects displayed such symptoms as exhaustion, apathy, depression, blackout, tension, palpitations, and confusion.

It is by no means rare for an individual so affected by the weather to be put into an alternate state of consciousness by an oncoming storm. Dutch researcher Solco Tromp has studied the effects of weather and concludes "there is hardly an organ of the human body which escapes the effects of changes in meteorological environment, and these effects are reflected either directly or indirectly in the mental processes of man." It therefore seems very likely that the thunderstorm was indeed somehow linked to Liberato's astonishing experience.

Witches into wolves
A depiction of the medieval folklore belief that witches could transform into wolves at night.

UNRELIABLE WITNESSES

The witchcraft mania that swept across Europe from the 15th to the 17th centuries, and even crossed the seas to America, brought about the deaths of at least 200,000 people. So-called witches were put to death by judges who sincerely believed that the accused had made a contract with the devil.

Devil's marks

The judges had little concrete evidence. But they did have abundant testimony by witnesses. Witches would often confess to their supposed crimes, sometimes under torture but often freely. The witch hunters also sought marks such as birthmarks and moles on their victims' bodies, which they saw as signs that the devil had branded them as his own. Today many abductees claim to have been marked in the same way by aliens.

A witch hunter's tools of torture

Taken at face value, these stories have a certain logic. The behavior of the abducting aliens may not be easy to understand. But why should we expect to comprehend the motivations of beings from other civilizations, or other species?

But let us take the skeptical view and assume that these experiences do not occur as they are reported. Diverse theories abound among ufologists, psychologists, and sociologists as to why people come up with such stories. Some, including French ufologist Bertrand Méheust, believe that UFO's are simply the product of the innermost workings of our minds, and projections of our own fantasies.

Witches claimed to be carried through the air to meetings with the devil.

Other researchers, including ufologist Leo Sprinkle, see UFO's as part of earth dwellers' cosmic education, with the extraterrestrials as our teachers. Or are UFO's perhaps some force that is entirely beyond our comprehension?

Bertrand Méheust has found themes in UFO and abduction reports that can be traced back to older traditions.

Witches claimed to be carried through the air to meetings with the devil. Abductees claim a similar experience when they are transported to alien spacecraft. The body marks found on abductees today are an echo of the centuries-old tradition of body marks found on suspected witches and people who had been "stolen by the fairies."

It does happen that some people who claim to see a UFO are unconsciously remembering a picture they have seen in a book or a story they

have heard. Yet there seems to be some form of collective agreement as to what an alien and its spacecraft should look like, which each witness varies.

Aliens, good or bad?

UFO encounters and alien abductions seem to run to a fairly standard pattern. However, no two experiences are exactly alike. Over the years the variety of UFO shapes has become so vast that they could fill a book without repetition.

The devil's disciple
A 17th-century English woodcut showing the devil marking a man as his follower.

Aliens, too, come in all shapes and sizes, and their attitude towards us also varies. Some contactees of previous decades — America's George Adamski, Italy's Eugenio Siragusa, France's Raël — believed themselves to be the privileged emissaries of an intergalactic parliament, or some other extraterrestrial power.

Different worlds, different species

Others find aliens less sympathetic. They are seen either as unscrupulous, using us earth dwellers as a farmer makes use of his livestock, or even on occasion actively malevolent, as though they have sinister designs to invade or take over our planet. If extraterrestrials truly exist, then it is possible they come from many different worlds and different species.

But if psychologists who specialize in the social effects of UFO's are correct, then all encounter witnesses are writing their own script. And if we believe this to be the case, then what these individuals are actually encountering is not aliens from outer space, but projections of their own innermost hopes and fears.

ADVERTISING PLANES

Do people want to see UFO's? It would appear that an increasing number do. But how much of what witnesses believe they have seen is merely a figment of an imagination that is predisposed to see such things?

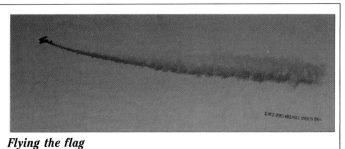
Flying the flag
An advertising plane over San Francisco.

"I CAN'T BELIEVE WHAT I'm seeing!" "No way is this is a plane!" "Hey, that's a flying saucer." These responses give the flavor of over a thousand UFO sightings analyzed by ufologist Allan Hendry in *The UFO Handbook* (1979).

But Hendry raised many doubts as to the authenticity of UFO sightings. For example, he gathered 11 sketches of UFO's drawn by witnesses. Each one is a "classic" flying saucer, a discoid or domed shape with a ring of flashing lights — typical of sketches drawn by witnesses in hundreds of accepted UFO cases. However, on investigation, each of the sketches was shown to be of nothing more otherworldly than an airplane trailing an advertising message in lights.

A row of flashing lights

What seems to have happened is that the witness saw something, failed to recognize what it was, and therefore altered it, adding details and attributes that transformed it into something recognizable. Hendry showed that virtually the only correct detail in the witnesses' drawings was the row of flashing lights, which really did exist on the advertising plane. The rest of the details — domes, trails of rocket exhaust, even seeing extraterrestrials inside the spacecraft — were added by each witness's imagination.

Saucers at sunset
The UFO's that prompted these eyewitness sketches (right) all turned out to be advertising planes. This photograph (left), also of an advertising plane, was taken at sunset in New Zealand, in 1980. The closeup (below) shows how the lights used to spell out the advertising message could be misinterpreted as a flying saucer.

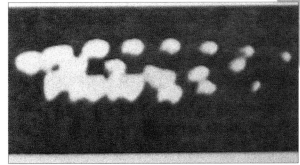

THE COLLECTIVE UNCONSCIOUS

Carl Gustav Jung

Swiss psychologist and psychiatrist Carl Gustav Jung wrote *A Modern Myth of Things Seen in the Sky* in 1958, a few years after the age of the flying saucer had begun. Jung doubted that flying saucers were real, but he was certain that they represented something of deep significance. He recognized the importance of looking beneath the surface of witness accounts. Jung noted that investigators were fond of saying how the witness was cool, rational, and not known to have a lively imagination, and therefore above suspicion of fabricating the whole episode.

However, Jung knew from his clinical work that these people are precisely those who might break out in an unexpected way. This is because their tightly controlled subconscious has to resort to extreme measures to get its message to the conscious mind. The mind projects a fantasy that is real to the person who is experiencing it. The mind does this "by extrapolating its contents into an object, which then mirrors what had lain hidden in the unconscious."

Jung saw the fantasy of flying saucers as just another example of this process. He knew how dreams, myths, and religions are means by which people all the world over cope with conflicts through wish fulfillment. For many people, this is a way of coping with a real world that may be somewhat harsher than they would like.

IMAGINARY UFO's

Alvin Lawson

In 1977 Alvin Lawson, a professor of English, conducted an experiment at a hospital in Anaheim, California, to discover how completely fictional accounts would compare with the accounts of people who claimed to have been abducted by aliens. His experiment is arguably one of the most important conducted on paranormal phenomena. Sixteen volunteers "who knew little of and cared less about UFO's," were each hypnotized and taken, step by step, through a typical abduction sequence — perceiving a UFO; being taken on board; describing the interior of the spacecraft; being "examined" by the occupants; and so on.

What the investigators expected to get was: "garbage — an amalgam of TV, film, sci-fi and UFO lore from media and myth." This would provide the investigators with a means of distinguishing "real" accounts from phoney ones. Lawson was astonished to find virtually

no difference between the accounts given by the actual and the imaginary abductees. Both told of bright, pulsating lights; of "floating" from one location to another, often passing through solid walls or floors; of paralysis; of being taken into a big, brightly lit room; and many lesser details.

Lawson claimed that this experiment revealed that we all — though we may have no conscious interest in UFO's — have within us the potential to fabricate an abduction story that is indistinguishable from the accounts of those who claim to have been abducted.

However, the participants in the experiment did differ in one regard from those who claimed to have experienced a close encounter of the third kind.

FICTION AND FOLKLORE

Bertrand Méheust

In 1978, French ufologist Bertrand Méheust shook the ufological world with *Science Fiction and Flying Saucers*. In this book he drew attention to the astonishing parallels between what is being reported today by UFO witnesses, and what had been written half a century earlier by science-fiction authors. For example, in 1957, a young illiterate Brazilian farmer claimed that he had an intimate encounter with a female alien. It seems unlikely that he could have read a sci-fi story written in 1930 — and which was only published in France — that describes in exact detail an identical encounter.

In a second book, *Flying Saucers and Folklore*, in 1985, Méheust demonstrated that the same was true of folklore beliefs. For example, he noted that in Scandinavian and Germanic mythology, sickness after meeting a folklore entity (such as fairies or ogres) is commonly reported. There is even a special word (*krasa* in Swedish) for the nausea, headaches, and body marks one must expect in an encounter with an otherworldly being. In today's UFO-related encounter cases, precisely the same effects are being reported.

Méheust's findings, like Jung's, encourage us to question the face value abductee reports. If Méheust is right, present-day abduction witnesses are in fact creating their own science fiction.

ALTERED STATES

Hilary Evans

Many UFO experiences take place, not in the physical world, but in the fantasy world of individuals who are temporarily in an alternate state of consciousness, argues Hilary Evans, a British ufologist. In past centuries, people who had hallucinatory or other such visionary experiences were supposed either to have been granted a heavenly vision or to be possessed by a malevolent demon. In modern times doctors offered a simpler, more scientific alternative: such people were mentally ill.

Today, this view is seen as being inaccurate in a large number of cases. It is recognized that people can be switched into alternate states by many conditions — fear, stress, defective diet, drugs and intoxicants. Many UFO sightings and abduction experiences occur to people driving alone or with a close companion, late at night on a quiet road. Such conditions seem most likely to induce alternate states.

Those who participated in the laboratory experiment were always aware that they had been fantasizing. For the real abductees, the memory of their experience produced very strong and often painful emotions as if they were memories of things that really happened.

The stories presented Lawson with a further puzzle: why do both sets of abduction stories share so many similar features? Lawson concluded that both groups of narrators are drawing on the same source that each of us shares — the subconscious memories of our birth. He found many similarities between the encounter experience and the birth experience: the fetuslike space beings, the passage through a tunnel, the sudden emergence into light, and so on.

PHYSICAL PHENOMENA

Few researchers believe that UFO's are nuts-and-bolts spacecraft. On the other hand, they cannot all be the product of invention or hallucination. Recent research suggests that they may have natural causes.

NE OF THE MOST common explanations for many UFO reports is that they are sightings of natural phenomena known to science, such as clouds, planets, meteorites, and unusual light effects, but seen in circumstances that make them difficult to identify. Other UFO's may be natural phenomena not known to science. Various such phenomena have been suggested, but the best researched are those that may be produced by geophysical events such as earthquakes. Experts in this field suggest that these phenomena may trigger a physiological response in the witness, which may in turn lead to a psychological experience such as hallucination.

Earthquake lights
As evidence that this process occurs, Dr. Michael Persinger, professor of psychology at Laurentian University, Sudbury, Ontario, claims that the number of UFO reports frequently increases weeks or months before a seismic event such as an earthquake. This suggests that some UFO sightings, at least, are associated with the tectonic strain within the earth's crust that precedes the event. According to Persinger, this strain creates short-lived luminosities (balls of light), which then stimulate the witness to hallucinate UFO's.

Research in Japan has confirmed that earthquakes can produce unusual lights, and these have been photographed. It is a scientific fact that rocks under pressure can produce radio waves. There is also plenty of documentary evidence, some of it dating back many centuries, of the mysterious appearance of small, mobile balls of light. Recent work by researchers such as Harley Rutledge and Paul Devereux has proved their existence, too. Persinger's theory links these sightings with the larger phenomenon of earthquake lights.

Fantastic events
Persinger's offering of a scientifically based and testable theory has been welcomed, but the figures on which his theory is based are questionable. However, if we accept provisionally that such geophysical events occur, his second proposition — that the luminous shapes may be perceived by the witness as a UFO and generate an encounter story — offers an interesting explanation of how apparently fantastic events may be brought about by mundane causes.

Dr. Michael Persinger

BLINDED BY THE LIGHT
Canadian professor of psychology Dr. Michael Persinger asserts that balls of light can be produced by the pressure on the earth's crust that causes earthquakes. Because of the nature of the energy that produces these luminosities, he says that a person encountering one might suffer "a variety of potentially hazardous biological and behavioral changes."

Paralysis and chest pain
These may include paralysis, tingling sensations, and chest pain. At close quarters, the phenomenon's magnetic fields would affect brain function and so alter consciousness, powers of perception, and memory.

A state of terror
The witness would be in a state of terror and might see auras such as those experienced during an epileptic fit. At even closer range, he or she would undergo severe electric shock, possibly losing consciousness, followed by amnesia. Physical contact, according to Persinger, would lead to burning and charring.

These symptoms and effects are very similar to those described by and medically diagnosed in people claiming to be UFO abductees.

Natural effects
This photograph was taken by the astronauts on board the space shuttle Discovery. *It shows a thundercloud lit from within by a flash of lightning. It demonstrates what dramatic and impressive effects nature is capable of displaying.*

Uncanny escorts
This artist's reconstruction shows "foo-fighters" as they appeared to airmen flying over Europe near the end of the Second World War. These phenomena have never been satisfactorily explained.

Contemporary photograph, 1944

"FOO-FIGHTERS"

While flying over Germany in 1944, U.S. Army Air Forces pilot Bill Leet reported a luminous sphere that suddenly appeared alongside his B-17 bomber "like a light switch being turned on." It stayed with the plane for about 45 minutes, then suddenly was gone. Leet said: "Our gunners wanted to shoot it down, but I ordered them not to. I told them if it was hostile, it would already have shot us down. Let's just try to figure out what it is, I told them."

No radar image

This was just one of many sightings of UFO's reported by Allied aircraft flying over Europe in the winter of 1944-45. Christened "foo-fighters" by the fliers, the discs and globes were up to about five feet in diameter and were usually seen at night. Sometimes they changed color from orange to red to white, and back to orange. They did not show up on radar screens.

After the war, the German and Japanese air forces admitted that they had been perplexed by the same type of phenomena.

Persinger describes the possible immediate biobehavioral effects of encountering such a ball of light as vertigo, noises in the head, dreamlike sequences, and "out-of-body" experiences. Later the witness might develop migraine, amnesia, nausea, physical exhaustion, enhanced suggestibility, and the symptoms of severe electric shock. These in turn could lead to long-term personality changes, perhaps characterized by religious awe, a compulsion to spread a message, emotional disorders, and modifications of memory from before the event. Specific details of these effects would be supplied from the witness's own cultural background and personal beliefs.

Meteorological conditions

This horrifying catalog is consistent with many stories told by encounter witnesses; Persinger's suggestion is plausible. But these effects may be brought about by other means. Tectonic luminosities may indeed be responsible — but we have already seen that meteorological conditions may have a similar effect, and there are other possible triggers.

Unfortunately, because encounter experiences so often happen to individuals on their own, it is difficult to extract from their often confused accounts what, if anything, triggered the event. But almost every story starts with the description of a bright light, and it is

possible that that light could be a luminosity such as Persinger describes. But it could also be light from a spaceship.

In 1947 pilot Kenneth Arnold made his classic UFO sighting in the Cascade Range, Washington State. Nearby, in the rough, inaccessible terrain of the Yakima Indian reservation, over 200 anomalous lights have been reported in the last 20 years. Researcher Greg Long says the reports include "stories of discs and cylinders, strange fires and glowing canyons, underground sounds, incidents of objects chasing automobiles and aircraft, radio system blackouts, encounters with humanoids, and a host of other strange occurrences."

Most descriptions, however, are of bright white lights moving low in the sky. Some are more specific: In 1978, a witness reported an egg-shaped object with an illuminated row of square

---

Sometimes the objects appear to be aware of human activity.

---

windows; in the center of the object lights of many colors swelled and surged like a beating heart. Sometimes the objects appear to be aware of human activity: In 1974, a couple observed three lights, red, blue, and yellow, arranged in a triangle; they believed that the lights were beckoning them. Two farmers reported that their tractors malfunctioned in the vicinity of a UFO. Dogs and horses have been noticed behaving unusually at the times the lights are seen.

There are striking parallels between these sightings and other cases in which UFO's looking like balls of light have been reported. The events at Yakima are similar to those reported by the English researcher Paul Devereux, by Professor Harley Rutledge from his Project Identification at Piedmont, Missouri, and by Project Hessdalen in Norway.

At all these locations, the lights have been photographed on hundreds of occasions, as well as observed with various scientific instruments. This has enabled investigators to make educated estimates as to their speed, size, and light intensity. Yet their physical and chemical makeup remains unknown.

Another interesting point is that while amateur observers claim to see objects with discernible shapes, flashing lights, and other flying-saucer-type features, the photographs taken by the investigators of these objects have been shown to be lights, and nothing more.

A challenge to science
Even considered as lights alone, however, these phenomena throw down a genuine challenge to science. There is nothing we know of at present that fits the description of these lights. They last longer than any known transient luminous phenomena such as earthquake lights or ball lightning. They are totally silent. They have been observed traveling over distances of several miles, proving that they are not associated with any specific site.

Some of them have been photographed with a background of mountains; this proves that they are not celestial bodies, mirages, or strange refraction effects. They are also larger

and brighter than any known atmospheric light. Equally puzzling are the "spook lights," which, under different names, are found in many parts of the world. The Brown Mountain Lights of North Carolina have been observed since at least 1771 — which means that car, train, and aircraft lights can be ruled out as explanations. These lights, about 20 inches in diameter, appear near the ground. They are intensely bright, and often reported to make a sizzling noise.

These luminosities undoubtedly exist in the physical world. But there is also evidence that they may respond to stimuli such as lasers, light, and radio waves — as well as telepathic messages.

Could it be that these balls of light, combining a physical existence with the ability to interreact with the human mind, hold the key to the UFO enigma?

Will-o'-the-wisp
The light phenomenon known variously as will-o'-the-wisp, ignis fatuus, and feu follet has been well known for some time, as this 19th-century cartoon shows. Such balls of light are generally associated with marshy areas; so it seems plausible that they are caused by marsh gas igniting and being carried by the wind. But it is intriguing that many witnesses assert that (as reflected in this cartoon) such phenomena appear to behave intelligently.

PROJECT IDENTIFICATION
In 1973 sightings of mysterious balls of light were reported in the hills around Piedmont, Missouri. Harley Rutledge, a physics professor from Southeast Missouri State University, was challenged by his students to explain them, and set up Project Identification to gather data. In seven years of investigation, 178 anomalous objects were recorded on 157 separate occasions.

Project Identification involved a team of 40 scientists, using a wide range of expensive equipment. Apart from telescopes, a selection of sophisticated cameras, and a spectrum analyzer, a gravimeter was used to measure changes in the earth's gravitational field.

Simultaneous observation from widely separated posts allowed the course, speed, and position of the objects to be determined. All sightings that had obvious explanations — such as aircraft, satellites, meteorites, headlights, streetlights, and refraction effects — were eliminated from the investigation.

Intelligent lights?
The most startling discovery of the project was that, on at least 32 recorded occasions, the movement of the object synchronized with the actions of the observers. Objects appeared to respond to a light being switched on and off, to a verbal or radio message, and even to an unspoken thought in the mind. Such claims, made by an ordinary member of the public, might be dismissed as fantasy; coming from Harley Rutledge, a professor of physics, they merit consideration.

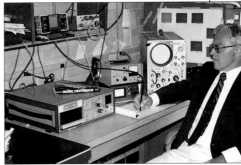

Harley Rutledge
At the end of the project, Rutledge was convinced that the behavior of at least some of the mysterious lights had been influenced by the actions of the team of observers.

Moving light photographed at Piedmont

Project Identification official report

IDENTIFIED FLYING OBJECTS

The majority of all recorded UFO sightings are eventually identified. A small percentage of these identified flying objects are deliberate hoaxes. But most are simply the result of observers innocently misinterpreting the appearance of unusual but perfectly natural phenomena.

Mistaken identity
The formation of lenticular, or lens-shaped clouds, frequently produces erroneous reports of UFO's. Several clouds lying one above another can create the impression of a "pile of saucers." Though rarely seen, these bizarre shapes remain stationary for long periods of time.

Storm cloud at sunset

UFO impostors
Clouds are commonplace. Yet every now and then their shape and behavior are so unusual that witnesses are startled into believing that they have seen a strange, solid object in the sky.

This spectacular cloud formation appeared in the hazy half-light just after sunset. From a distance, and with poor visibility, it is easy to understand how the eye of an untrained observer could mistake this irregularly shaped cloud for something altogether more sinister.

Lenticular clouds over Alaska

Funnel vision
When the sky darkened during a heavy summer storm, the citizens of Cleveland, Ohio, witnessed the formation of an exceedingly strange funnel-shaped feature at the base of a bank of clouds.

Altocumulus cloud

A sky monster?
Although this is a particularly unusual shape, altocumulus clouds often appear as rounded individual masses. This bulbous yet beautiful cloud appeared over the rolling hills of the North Wales countryside.

Summer storm with a funnel-shaped cloud

A flying saucer!

IFO's in the Antarctic

Numerous photographs exist of odd, saucer-shaped clouds forming over the vast expanse of Antarctica. Although these pictures have been proved to show only clouds, some people still want to believe that alien spacecraft fly periodically over the Antarctic. They even claim that this is because alien bases already exist in the region.

Dawn display, Antarctica

Meteor mistakes

Witnesses all over the globe have described seeing "cigars" or "saucers" in the sky. Many of these UFO sightings could in fact be the result of meteors and space debris entering the earth's atmosphere. The mistake is not difficult to make: the conventional image of meteors simply falling to earth is false. They can actually appear to travel in any direction, including upward. Confusion is compounded by the fact that meteors can be of any color, even green!

Illustration of a near miss

Optical illusion

Rainbow effects

This dazzling display of iridescence sometimes occurs at dusk when a cloud appears high in the stratosphere and is illuminated by the sun while the rest of the sky remains dark. To the untrained eye, and with a little imagination, it could look like a brightly lit alien spacecraft, drifting through a twilight sky.

Iridescent "mother-of-pearl" clouds

A UFO mirage

Some of the most startling visions of UFO's are actually mirages. A layer of cold air trapped beneath a layer of hot air will refract light passing between the two. This bending of light alters the visible position of an object. A star or planet can appear in the wrong part of the sky, or even be seen when it should not be visible at all. The effect is heightened by atmospheric conditions that can distort the image, making it appear as a huge glowing ball, often flashing and repeatedly changing color.

Planetary sightings

Stars and planets stimulate the greatest number of false UFO reports, and these are often the easiest to disprove. The photograph below shows, from top to bottom, Jupiter, Saturn, Venus, and the Moon. The real champion is Venus. This planet can appear over a hundred times brighter than its neighbors, and has been described as "resembling an aircraft's landing light aimed head-on in the daylight." The refraction of light from these heavenly bodies can produce strange patterns in the sky, and some unusual effects, including rapid sequences of colors (the most common being red, white, and blue), and even an illusion of movement. When these are combined, witnesses have claimed not only that they could see a strange flying object, but that it had multicolored flashing lights and was rotating.

Half-moon in daylight

Tricks of the light

The sun and moon are the most familiar of all heavenly bodies. Yet even they are sometimes mistaken for UFO's. Fog, mist, ice crystals, clouds, and snow can distort images and fool the unwary. Some historians think that it was the illusion of a shimmering cross in the sky that converted the Roman emperor Constantine the Great to Christianity in A.D. 312.

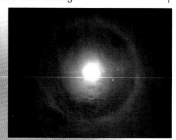

Halos around the sun

Beaded lightning

The moon and three planets in the night sky

Lightning illusions

Most of us have seen the common forked lightning and are used to it. But other more unusual varieties have spawned many UFO reports. Types that could cause confusion include beaded, ribbon, and ball lightning.

Fire in the sky

Many people have gazed in wonder at the fabulous spectacle of the auroras and some have attributed them to the actions of creatures from other worlds. But scientists have provided a much less fanciful explanation. The magnetic fields high above the North and South Poles funnel charged atomic particles downward until they meet and excite atoms in the upper air. It is these atoms that cause the flashing lights of the auroras. Oxygen atoms produce red, yellow, and green lights; nitrogen produces green too, as well as violet and blue.

Aurora borealis — the northern lights

***Sundog seen
in Alaska***

Ice crystals in the air
Under certain conditions,
thousands of tiny ice crystals can
be suspended in the atmosphere.
When sunlight travels through this
myriad of airborne frozen
droplets, a phenomenon known as
a sundog can occur. (Other names
for this effect are "mock sun,"
"parhelion," or "moondog," if the
moon is the light source.) The ice
crystals form hexagonal prisms,
and the reflected light gathers
into impressive radial patterns.

***Antarctic
sundog***

IDENTIFIED FLYING FAKES
Many convincing photographs of UFO's have been
proved by experts to be hoaxes. Several tests now
exist to help detect fakes, whether intentional or
otherwise. For example, analysis of lighting conditions
and film imagery can detect accidental effects such as
lens flare. The study of film defects can reveal double
exposures, as can overlapping images, where areas of
the background partially obscure foreground features.
Other tests include edge enhancement, color
contouring, and digital image enhancement.

Flying hubcap
*This infamous picture was taken
in Bakersfield, California, by a
photographer who has since
confessed to creating a hoax.*

Photographic tricks
*These nocturnal tracks
of lights over Honolulu
could easily be faked in
the darkroom. Long
exposures can record
moving lights over a
period of time. At night
car headlights, or
even streetlights
photographed from a
moving camera, can
look like encounters
with alien craft.*

Double exposure
*The superimposition of
one photographic image
on top of another can
produce quite dramatic
effects. An object can
be made to appear on
any chosen background.
This "spirit light" has
been created simply by
placing a circular blob
of white light against a
churchyard background.*

IS THERE ANYBODY OUT THERE?

NY SCHOOLCHILD CAN DRAW you a picture of an alien spaceman – even though there is no convincing evidence that aliens have visited earth, or even that they exist at all. But an image of extraterrestrial beings exists, regardless of reality.

In the same way, most people have a mental image of what a UFO is. They immediately start to think in terms of extraterrestrial spacecraft, and may describe a cigar-shaped "mother ship," a disc-shaped "scout ship," or some other generally accepted form.

UFO's with a basis in fact

This preconception is unfortunate because it undermines serious debate of a serious subject. For although the concept of alien spacemen is speculative, it is a fact that strange moving objects occasionally appear in our airspace. At Yakima in Washington State, Piedmont in Missouri, and Hessdalen in Norway, phenomena have been seen that so far defy explanation. These may not be the only UFO's to have a basis in fact, but they are the only ones for which we have, here and now, photographs and data from scientific instruments. The eminent Swiss psychologist and psychiatrist, Carl Gustav Jung, described flying saucers as "a modern myth of things seen in the skies." This is a good definition – if by "myth" we mean a consensus image of something whose existence is uncertain. There is a myth about alien spacemen; there is a myth about UFO's, how they look and how they behave.

Sifting the evidence

For a balanced approach to the subject, it is important that we remember how much of the UFO story depends on human testimony, and how little on objective fact. This does not mean that we should dismiss witness reports as worthless. It merely indicates that we should examine all testimonies very thoroughly.

When there is no alternative explanation for a sighting, a UFO may indeed be the best working hypothesis. But we have seen that there are different ways of interpreting most, perhaps all, UFO stories. The more mundane explanations generally have no concrete evidence either; we just have to decide which is the more probable interpretation.

Jung spoke of a "modern" myth. He reminded us that flying saucers are

essentially of our own time, but a multitude of signs and visions have been documented as appearing in the skies since the dawn of recorded history. It is from the skies that the threat of destruction is most feared. It is to the skies that we look for salvation. It may be that alien spacecraft are age-old myths recycled in an up-to-date form.

For centuries humankind has dreamed of leaving this planet. Now, at last, we have taken the first tentative steps into space. Science has helped us predict what we may find, but we still cannot answer the most fundamental of questions: Will we discover other beings like ourselves in the cosmos?

Are we alone?
Many people think it probable that extraterrestrial UFO's were invented by the human imagination because we want to believe that we are not alone. We seize on any scrap of information that may justify that belief. But although the evidence may have been misinterpreted in this way, it is not necessarily invalid. UFO's, of a sort, undoubtedly exist. They may not teach us anything about beings from other worlds, but they can certainly show us just how much we have to learn about our own.

INDEX

PHOTOGRAPHIC SOURCES —

Abacus Books/Mark Harrison: 109br; **The Aetherius Society**: 31cl, 113t (© 1990); **Associated Press**: 52c, bl; **Aviation Photo International/J. Flack**: 49cr, 50tr; **Aviation Picture Library**: 129t; **The Bettmann Archive**: 62tl, 63b, 70t, bl, 96t; **Bridgeman Art Library**: 25b; **J.E. Bulloz**:128t; **Camera Press**: 49t; **Jean-Loup Charmet**: 33tr; **Bruce Coleman Ltd.**: 51cr (H. Reinhard); **Philip Daly**: 36c, 37t, 81tl, cl; **Courtesy of John S. Derr, U.S. Geological Survey**: 122b; **Mary Evans Picture Library**: 32t, b, 33br, 36b, 37c, 40l, br, 41tl, tr, c, 45c, br, 50tl (D. Stacy), 58tc, 65tl, tr, 71tl, tr, 72bl, 73tl, tr, bl, 74c, 84b, 102t, 104, 120-1 (ephemera), 122t, 123c, b, 125r, 126c, 128c, 130tl, bl (Alvin Lawson), 131, 134, 135t, c & bl & br (H. Rutledge), 137cl, cr, 139cr, bl; **Werner Forman Archive**: 22tl; **Fortean Picture Library**: 30l, tr, 31tl, tc, tr, br, 32c (Llewellyn Publishing), 37b, 38t (Puforg), 39b, 44 (D. Stacy), 45l, tr, 48t, 48c & b (Puforg), 50-1 background (B. Skinner), 50b, 52tl, tr, bc, 53, 54tl, tr, br (P. Panton), 63t, 72tr, c, 73cr, br, 74t, 75tl, tr, 81cr (D. Stacy), 84t, 89tr, 103c (D. Stacy), 117c (D. Stacy), 133r (D. Stacy), 139br; **John Frost Collection**: 114-5 (newspapers); **Denis Gifford Collection**: 34-5 border ('Pete Mangan'/L. Miller & Son, 'Space Worlds'/Steamline, 'Sky Police Comics'/Cartoon Art Productions, 'Space Action'/Junior Books Inc.), 34tl (Reproduced with special permission of King Features Syndicate), r (DC Comics), 35br (DC Comics), 55b & 64b (© 1954 Fables Publishing Co. Inc., re © 1982 William M. Gaines), 75bl (Dell, 1967), br (Avon, 1950), 80t, b (Dell, 1967); **GSW Inc., Phoenix, Arizona**: 56-7 computer enhancements, 58t, cr, cl, bl, 116c; **Guardian Action International, Salt Lake City, Utah**: 108b, 109t; **Sonia Halliday**: 25t; **Robert Harding Picture Library**: 139t; **HarperTorchbooks Editions, illustration © 1964 Harper & Row Publishers Inc. Reprinted by permission of HarperCollins Publishers Inc.**: 109bl; **Michael Holford**: 24t, c, 28; **Rusty Hudson**: 17; **Hulton-Deutsch Collection**: 26t, 31bl (Fox); **Image Bank**: 42-3

& 56-7c (J. Rajs), 85b (K. Chernush); **Images Colour Library**: 22tr, c, 23ct, cb, 26b, 40t, 41bl; **Ted Seth Jacobs**: 103b; **Kobal Collection**: 27, 71b, 90, 91, 92, 93, 108t, c; **Dr. Rima E. Laibow**: 105c; **Frank Lane Picture Agency**: 136tr, br, 138c, br; **Mansell Collection**: 128b; **Dr. Jean Mundy**: 103t, 105t; **NASA**: 97cr; **Natural History Photographic Agency/J. Bain**: 41br; **Oxford Scientific Films/Doug Allan**: 137tl, tr, b, 139cl; **OSF/K. Westerkov**: 138tr; **Philip Panton**: 54bl; **Axel Poignant Archive**: 22bl; **Popperfoto**: 30cr, 31cr, 73bc, 74b, 89tl, 116t, b, 117t, b; **Press Association**: 51b; **Jenny Randles**: 129bl, bc; **Science Photo Library**: 22-3 background (NASA), 22br (ESA), 39t, 70br, 85t, 94l, 96b, 97t, cl, 124 (J. Sanford), 132 (NASA), 136tl (Dr. R. Spicer), 138bl (J. Sanford); **Simon & Schuster/P. Sher, FPG/A. Kearney**: 36t; **John Spencer**: 81tr; **Sphere Books/Terry Oakes**: 102b; **Frank Spooner Pictures/ Gamma**: 49cl (B. Markel), b (B. Riha), 64t (Kermani/Liaison), 81b & 88t (Apesteguy), 113b (B. Berger), 123t (S. Ferry/Liaison), 126t (Brissaud); **Syndication International**: 38b; **Topham Picture Source/AP**: 62tr; **TORRO Research Centre**: 50cl; **TRH Pictures**: 65b; **Unarius Academy of Science**: 112t, b; **Virgin Atlantic Airlines**: 55c; **Virgin Group Ltd.**: 55t; **Zefa**: 136bl, 138tl (P. Freytag), 140-1 (J. Ballard); **Department of Prints & Drawings, Zentralbibliothek, Zurich**: 24b, 126b.

b - bottom; c - center; t - top; r - right; l - left.

Efforts have been made to contact the holder of the copyright for each picture. In several cases these have been untraceable, for which we offer our apologies.